SECULAR EVA

# SECULAR EVANGELISM

FRED BROWN

SCM PRESS LTD

TO MURIEL
WITH GRATITUDE

334 01475 1 (paper)
334 01474 3 (cloth)

First published 1970
by SCM Press Ltd
56 Bloomsbury Street London WC1

© SCM Press Ltd 1970

Printed in Great Britain by
Northumberland Press Limited
Gateshead

# CONTENTS

*Publisher's Note*

The author, a Salvation Army officer, has written this book in a private capacity and not as an official representative of the Salvation Army.

If theology would avoid the dangers of a false secularization the sure safeguard is to keep at its heart the essential Christian attitudes of creature to Creator, of sinner to Saviour. It is when we have lost the attitude of the worshipper, of awe and reverence in the presence of the Other, and when we have ceased to ask forgiveness for our sins, that the line has been crossed. It is on this line that the crisis for secular Christianity is located.

*God, Christ and the World* by A. M. Ramsey

Why are we so reluctant to admit and teach a new vocabulary of divine revelation? It could be that by attempting to bulldoze adolescent minds into orthodoxy of belief we are innocently trampling upon the face of God and making it more difficult for earnest seekers after truth to be real persons.

Surely the church's great mission in secular society is to help people to understand their unconscious spirituality; to perceive the nature of God's presence and activity in the world; to find a greater measure of true fulfilment by consciously co-operating with God whom, I repeat, they already know by some other name.

Chapter 2 of the present book

# I

# Secular Man and the Gospel

Britain is in the grip of revolution. Not only are unprecedented strides being made in the realms of science and technology, but every fundamental moral and spiritual assumption is being questioned, sometimes drastically modified, and not infrequently discarded altogether. These convulsions of change are to be welcomed, not feared or interpreted as signs of rebellion against God. For he is in the world and speaking to his people sometimes through the very changes they themselves resist and condemn. He is redemptively at work at every point of tension, conflict, and turmoil. To turn our back to the world is to turn away from God. Yet some of us, calling ourselves evangelicals, motivated by the noblest intentions, are doing just this in the name of religion. We view secular and permissive society as our call to rearguard action, meaning separation from the world and fastidious adherence to traditional evangelical terminology. On a number of occasions, sharing with older Christians my bewilderment at not being able to communicate my faith in God to modern man, I have been advised to stick to proven ways and words. 'Preach the old truths,' they have urged. 'Talk about Jesus and the people will come' (meaning come to evangelical meetings). 'Hold up the Cross; preach the Blood.' 'Call people to repent and be saved.' When I have asked for evidence that this was being done effectually anywhere in Britain they have vaguely mentioned isolated churches of this denomination or that; and ignored the vast majority of churches and chapels where, despite the ministries of dedicated men and women, numbers are falling off and the general situation is one of chronic disappointment and bewilderment; or they have claimed that because this was *not* being done, the present *malaise* in the total church was inevitable, and proved their point.

What these devout supporters of traditional expressions of evangelism fail to recognize is that secularism makes God himself expendable, a luxury at best for individuals that way inclined.

To bemoan the new paganism of Britain and insist that people should be prepared to listen to the gospel because it alone meets their basic needs is as useless as trying to sell binoculars in a school for the blind. People are not interested. It serves no purpose to condemn them or to continue talking in terms they do not understand; no purpose, that is, apart from possibly placating the conscience of the would-be evangelist.

Nevertheless, we evangelicals, or far too many of us, continue to prepare for operations as though life had stood still for fifty years. We engage in dialogues, teach-ins, conferences and endless talking by other names to improve our existing forms of evangelism. Clearly we believe that once we have learned how to streamline our presentation, modernize our techniques of communication, people will listen to our message and respond. The assumption is often made, for instance, that our open-air meetings are largely ignored because the meetings themselves are not well enough conducted. The need is for more prayerful preparation and skilful leadership, for music that people know and enjoy, for a vocabulary related to everyday life, for efficiency, conciseness and topicality. Get these things right and – we are assured – the desired success will automatically follow. It's true, of course, that such matters sometimes require urgent attention, but no degree of improvement along this line alone will touch the basic problem – secularism on a growing scale.

Someone has said – I think it was D. T. Niles of Ceylon – that evangelism is one beggar telling other beggars where to find food. Painful experience, however, has taught me that sometimes I have created problems for people by zealously telling them not where to find bread, but how to make it for themselves from my rather dogmatic recipe. They have tried, only to be disappointed and even resentful. It seems to me that one of the main responsibilities of the Christian church is to tell people where to find bread, and then to let them find it for themselves. If we stuff them with bread baked exclusively in our particular denominational oven, then, despite our sincerity, they will probably be nauseated and develop an allergy. This has already happened with thousands of young people who have rejected the institution of the church and thereby, unknowingly, turned their backs upon the truth that makes men free. That word *free* focuses the irony of the situation. We proclaim a gospel that offers freedom, and yet are ourselves enslaved within a system of words, structures, traditions, dogmas and creeds. These things are, of course, important but only as signposts and never as destinations. By making them destinations we are guilty of idolatry, the end result of which is always disastrous.

The crucial question we have to face is how to communicate the gospel to secular man. Is there common ground between him and the committed Christian? For evangelicals who believe that the only or the main answer is an intensification of existing programmes of outreach, there is little to interest them in this book. My concern is to explore the possibility of finding new ways of making God meaningful today. The task, I readily confess, is beyond me, but I make the attempt of necessity in the light of hard experience in working at a busy Salvation Army centre in the West End of London.[1] Shortly after arriving there some six years ago, I realized that our traditional methods of evangelism, and more particularly our biblical vocabulary, were not getting through on the scale desired. Young people especially were mystified, when they were not indifferent. Their attitude, which I have tried to analyse in later chapters, compelled us to seek both a new approach and a new language. I did so, initially, with reluctance, fearful that I was on the wrong track completely and in danger of diluting our evangelical faith, but the situation finally was too urgent for further delay. Our work had driven us into close association with a wide cross-section of the community, including young drifters, drug abusers, flower children, angry crusaders without a cause, and a growing number of moral and spiritual

[1] Opened in 1882 by William Booth, Regent Hall, the centre in Oxford Street, sometimes called the City Temple of the Salvation Army, was a roller-skating rink before its conversion. Its three Sunday meetings are attended by an aggregate of 1,000 people, many of whom are not officially affiliated with the Army. They also include Salvationist visitors to London, which means that virtually every meeting focuses the Army's internationalism.

casualties of our permissive society.

For most of them the Christian faith was wholly irrelevant, outdated and outgrown. They neither wanted it nor felt the need for it. Most of them did not even respect it. They had concluded that the church is archaic, reactionary, stuffy, against fun and freedom, on the side of the Establishment, and at best optional. It is certainly no longer a factor for serious consideration. I should explain – in case you think I am exaggerating the situation – that I write from within my experience of the inner city. It could be that village and town attitudes are different, that the provinces in general do not reflect the religious life and outlook of our major cities, notably London, but I believe that they will, well within the next ten years. Perhaps I should make it clear, too, that I do not share all the young people's criticisms, some of which express more ignorance than insight, and re-echo a general protest and rebellion against everything authoritarian. But the criticisms are real and, I believe, sincerely held by a growing number. More to the point, they will never be answered by patronage, condemnation or devout indignation.

It is my conviction that God is speaking to the church through the young people of this and other countries. I believe that their new-found freedom is of God the Holy Spirit. That freedom has not been given by their elders; the young people have taken it, sometimes inspired by the values that belong to God's kingdom. Youth is on the march, not on the side of the big battalions, but often with the despised minority fighting for moral values. I believe that God is using the rebellious, truculent, lovable, stupid, exasperating, irrepressible, desperately caring, sincere young people of today to challenge the Christian church to release on an ever broader front the truth that is centred in Christ and that expresses, sometimes in surprising ways, the perspective that gives life cohesion and direction. Unfortunately, many of us, indebted to the church and anxious to be faithful, spend too much time looking over our shoulders. Even if we venture a little on the merging boundaries of the church and the world, that seeming no-man's-land in which crucial theological battles are fought, we quickly clamour for the security of familiar thought-forms and esoteric practices. We scurry down the funk holes of orthodoxy in the name of defending the faith, of being true to our spiritual forefathers. But all too often our real motivation is fear; no, not fear, for that is honourable enough. It is cowardice, the spirit that mistakes bigotry for conviction, and shouts slogans to hide its paucity of thought.

We are in danger of being unfaithful to our spiritual forebears, but for reasons the opposite of the ones we imagine. We are allowing the fruits of their organizing skill to evolve into institutions which restrict rather than expand our evangelical enterprise. We are relegating God to a mausoleum, fearful that he will make the theological scene untidy by breaking free of our verbal embalming. We are giving our traditional way of doing things a divine mandate, and shouting futile protest at the rapidly changing ways of society. Our battle cry is safety first, whereas Jesus promised not safety, but security. No wonder we are afraid to take risks, to venture like Abraham into a far country of uncertainty and danger.

The time has come – is long overdue – for us to face reality, life as it is and not as we should like it to be. In the situation that faced us in the heart of London we inescapably had to decide what to do, though in reality there was only one thing we could do. Theoretically, we could have condemned the people concerned for not listening to our traditional presentation of the gospel and withdrawn; or we could have continued in the same old way, in the hope that one day they would understand. In fact, we tried the latter for some considerable time, until driven to admit that not only was our message utterly unintelligible to our hearers, but because of the way we were saying it they were rapidly reaching the conclusion that the Christian gospel itself, which we claimed to represent, was obviously not for them. The only answer was to find some better means of communicating our faith to them. We made the attempt, stimulated by the writings of Paul Tillich, John Robinson, Dietrich Bonhoeffer, and Harvey Cox. There were many other writers to whom we turned, of course, but I mention these four specifically because evangelicals tend to view them with suspicion and in some cases accuse them of being unfaithful to the essential Christian gospel. All I can testify is that their insights, ideas, and general teaching helped us considerably at the grass roots, in our personal relationships with people normally beyond the influence of organized religion.

We found that the gulf between us could be bridged, that we had a common language and were able to talk about Christian truth without giving the impression that it was unrelated to life as defined by secular man.

One final explanation. I am a Salvation Army officer, but this book reflects my own views and not necessarily official thinking or policy within the Salvation Army. There are, doubtless, numerous officers and soldiers who disagree with my ideas and tentative conclusions. It would be most surprising if in a movement like ours this were not the case. As with the church generally, we are in a state of ferment, which means that though the fundamentals of our faith retain our unanimous support we are engaged in healthy controversy about the best ways and means of fulfilling our God-given role in society. All of us recognize the futility of repeating parrot-fashion dearly beloved biblical and doctrinal phrases which, though still significant for us, are empty of meaning for the vast majority of people. On the other hand, we all deplore irresponsible comment which provokes to no purpose and shocks to the point of alienating dedicated people with different convictions. Our aim is to engage in open discussion, to share ideas and encourage exploration of what God is trying to say to us in these exciting days.

However, we are suspicious of the sort of talking that becomes a respectable substitute for the drudgery of costly involvement and experimentation. Pious verbosity wins paper victories, but leaves the real situation untouched and probably more obscure. My hope is that what follows will focus some of the right questions and move us a little nearer to one or two answers.

# Youthful Secularists

The Salvation Army bandsmen at Regent Hall in London's West
End represent many trades and professions. Some of them are
carpenters, clerks, builders, solicitors, executives, estate agents,
students and schoolteachers. One of the latter, head of the religious education department at a secondary modern school for boys,
invited me to teach the senior pupils. The idea was that on one
day a week I should commence immediately after school assembly
and for forty-minute periods throughout the whole day take different groups of, as it turned out, between nine and thirty-five teenagers.

My first day was unforgettable. I arrived in good time, all
'genned up' for what I confidently anticipated would be a fascinating discussion about the existence of God. Teaching by mono-
logue was out of the question. What we needed was discussion,
the healthy cut-and-thrust of debate! There was nothing to fear.
I knew all the classical arguments for the existence of God. Let
the boys throw their scepticism and cynicism, even their ridicule
at me. I was ready, well briefed – and innocent.

In case any well-intentioned schoolteacher imagines that the
basis of my mistaken notions was a desire to proselytize, I must
request that he refrain from casting his pearls, at least for the time
being. I was teaching religious education, not preaching or seeking
to indoctrinate. My aim was to pose questions rather than provide
answers, to tease slumbering adolescent minds into activity.

Sharp at nine-twenty I started with the first group, though
*started* is not strictly accurate. I was a non-starter from the first
word or at most the first sentence. The boys did not want to know.
They argued right enough; the discussion could not have been
livelier. But their disinterest in whether God existed or not was

painfully, though eloquently, articulated – sighs, yawns, occasional expletives, demands that we talk about real life, vehement
condemnations of the church, and references like hypocrites,
stuffed shirts, puritans and much else. The subject of God was a
closed book.

The following week the theme was not God but personal
relationships – boy meets girl and the rest. The forty minutes were
barely enough. I continued for two terms. Pressure of other work
finally compelled me to withdraw, but I was reluctant to do so
largely for reasons of self-interest. The boys were teaching me
more than I was teaching them. Probably it would be more correct
to say that they were confirming my worst suspicions – that in
the lives of most modern young people there is a God-blank. What
really surprised me was the matter-of-fact way in which the vast
majority of the boys took for granted that the whole subject of
God was beside the point. Their summing-up was crystal clear:
suppose there is a God – so what! They said this without vindic-
tiveness or any other sort of passion. God, exist or not, was irrelevant, a bore, a waste of time.

This was secularism all right, as thoughtless as it was final. Yet
the boys themselves – not all of them, but most of them – believed
implicitly in many of the values of God's kingdom as taught by
the church. They believed in Christian compassion and in some
cases illustrated that quality to a remarkable extent; but they
objected to the Christian label. It was unnecessary. They simply
liked helping people, and that was all there was to it. Why drag
God or Christ or the church into a perfectly straightforward
situation of lending a hand? Anybody decent would do it. No need
to go to church!

These schoolboys were unconscious secularists or well on their
way in that direction. When I was their age, some thirty years ago,
I and my contemporaries were also reluctant to attend church,
to pray or to read the Bible. Religion represented for us a world
reserved for old people. No self-respecting man, especially if he
was fourteen or so years of age, wanted openly to be associated
with anything remotely religious. But we all took for granted the
existence of God, the fact of God, the menacing presence of God.

I am not writing of grammar and public schoolboys with
university potential; they have doubtless always argued about

metaphysics and passed through phases of atheism, agnosticism and most other 'isms'. The boys I have in mind attended secondary modern schools. In general terms they were not academic, bookish or given to philosophical or theological argument. I certainly was not, and I was one of their number. But in so far as it is possible for such adolescents to believe in God, we believed. Not that our belief made any real difference to our living. But it was the background to life that we took for granted.

God was not a factor in our experience but he was there. He did not intrude, but he did exist. It was right and proper to believe in him. Some people, distinguishable by their dark clothing, not to mention their pained expression, took him very seriously and tried to make us do likewise. They did not succeed, but not once did it cross our minds that the God, whose devoted servants self-evidently they were, did not exist. Frequently we wished that they did not exist, but they were as real as he was, and equally as tedious. Our atheism was practical but not theoretical. God was not dead. He merely slumbered at a safe distance, and we were grateful to leave it at that.

Our modern counterparts think otherwise. For them, too, God is not dead; he never was. They are emancipated from such nonsense. And if perchance a few of their elders persist in their superstitions, picking over discredited ideas and dogmas, no matter. Time will painlessly bear away the last remnants of a dead or dying cult.

If this impression given to me by a hundred secondary modern schoolboys in London is only a pointer – the indication of a tendency – of youthful thinking in Britain, we must ask what it means to the task of the church. Do we throw up our hands in despair? Or do we accept the situation and seek new ways, even a new language, to communicate the eternal message of God?

Such questions were brought into even sharper focus in our youth club. We opened it to cater for some of the hundreds of suburbanites who pour into London's Piccadilly and district, notably on Saturday nights. The history of the club is quite a story in itself, but this is not the time to tell it. What must be mentioned, however, is that through the club we met multitudes of young people who normally remain beyond the influence of organized or institutional religion. On the whole, they were simply older versions of the schoolboys.

They thought of God, in so far as they thought of him at all, as a refuge for the fearful and weak. Prayer was a substitute for work, a cowardly substitute at that. Hopes of life beyond represented escapism – an evasion of personal responsibility to remedy the wrongs of this life. They had no interest in any traditional definitions of God or of things associated with him. The young people had concluded that words like God, Holy Spirit, divine and faith symbolized unreality, a sort of fantasy world characterized by coloured glass windows and choirs singing meaningless dirges.

Any lingering doubts that secularism's conquest of modern youth was virtually complete were, however, shattered in a different setting altogether. We had been making real progress in establishing relationships with a sizable group of flower children. At the time, the cult was at its height of popularity, attracting growing numbers who either attached themselves to one of the many groups milling around in central London or formed a group of their own. The group with whom we became involved met every week-end in Hyde Park. Initially, they were suspicious, a polite understatement, but two of our youth leaders, despite their Salvation Army uniforms, were finally accepted unconditionally.

Nevertheless, I was surprised to receive a request from the flower children that we, the Salvation Army, and they should engage in serious dialogue. They suggested that each side should nominate three representatives who would be given the chance briefly to state a personal view, and be questioned by the other speakers; and that immediately afterwards anyone present should be allowed to address the whole company, subject to the discretion of the chairman, who, *they* insisted, should be a Salvation Army officer.

We arranged the dialogue for nine o'clock on Sunday night, thinking that by then our main hall would be available following the customary public meeting. Ten minutes before the deadline they started to arrive. Their clothing vividly illustrated why they called themselves flower children; they wore beads and bells; their eyes danced and never stopped smiling. The whole group, gay but serious, brought with them a spirit of infectious joy. They numbered 120.

Before this encounter, not really knowing personally any flower children, I had tended to put them all in the same category – one of anti-social behaviour, laziness, moral permissiveness, and experimentation with drugs. As I listened with growing incredulity, I realized that the majority of this group were ordinary, law-abiding, hard-working, responsible members of society who cared desperately about social justice, and wanted to put the world right. They cared. God, how they cared! But they wanted nothing to do with G-O-D, by which they meant organized religion.

For them secularism was axiomatic. They did not argue about it. It was self-evident. They accused us of pious irresponsibility. Of all people, we Christians were guilty of devout verbosity, making our endless talking a substitute for real caring. Their words hurt without giving offence.

The flower children, their colourful clothes and sombre words at times giving an impression of ludicrous incongruity, were too sincere and earnest to evoke from us anything but admiration and respect. That dialogue made a lasting impact on my thinking. I am not sure what the flower children made of it all, though they asked if they could come back, and did so on every Sunday night for eighteen months, but the influence of that first encounter lives with me still. Two impressions were outstanding. These young people shared many of our ideals, and gave priority to what can only be called spiritual values. For them love was infinitely more than sex; peace far more than the absence of war; joy more a quality of life than the result of favourable circumstances. But they never thought of these and other spiritual values in abstract terms; always in terms of people, of personal relationships.

We talked about loving God and our neighbour; they talked about loving their neighbour. We spoke of praying and making provision for the under-privileged, meaning the hungry; they impatiently dismissed the idea of praying in such circumstances and insisted that providing bread was all that mattered. These young people, it seemed to us, were sharing the perspective of Christ. Not for one moment did they think in such terms, but for all practical purposes the end result was the same.

The second outstanding impression was that these youngsters, the object of so much criticism, were unconsciously avoiding the danger of devout introspection. While Christians were tempted – put it no stronger than that – to feel their spiritual pulses in concern that they were not loving God enough; or working themselves up into a state of self-loathing to prove to God the extent of their repentance; or pleading with him to do something about the state of the world, these youthful secularists were defeating such pious self-centredness in the most obvious and effective way – thinking about people, especially the under-privileged. Perhaps I am over-simplifying. It would be foolish and beyond my intention to give the impression that all Christians are prone to chronic introspection, or that all flower children, certainly the ones who attended our dialogue and the weekly meetings afterwards, are free of self-centredness. But these general comments stand, if only as pointing to certain trends. We came to the conclusion that though the vast majority of these young people had rejected the institution of the church they had not rejected the Reality of whom the church in her best moments speaks clearly. They were committed to truth, justice, love, mercy, compassion and many of the other qualities and values that Christ both defined and exemplified. Conscious faith in him, however, was something they neither understood nor desired.

Nevertheless they know God, I believe, by some other name; experience his acceptance by their growing capacity to accept themselves and other individuals; respond to him by their fidelity to the things that harmonize with his nature; serve his kingdom by caring for people; discover him by exploring the depths of their own personalities.

Then why are we so reluctant to admit and teach a new vocabulary of divine revelation? It could be that by attempting to bull-doze adolescent minds into orthodoxy of belief we are innocently trampling upon the face of God and making it more difficult for earnest seekers after truth to be real persons.

Surely, the church's great mission in secular society is to help people to understand their unconscious spirituality; to perceive the nature of God's presence and activity in the world; to find a greater measure of true fulfilment by consciously co-operating with God whom, I repeat, they already know by some other name.

# 3

## *Christian Secularists*

What evidence is there that young secularists know God by some other name, and that by trapping him in rigid theological definitions we are making it more difficult for many of them to find him and to understand themselves? The urgency of the matter was brought home to me in a most surprising way. We initiated at Regent Hall a scheme similar to Voluntary Service Overseas and Community Service Volunteers. Young people were invited to help us on a full-time basis for periods of from six months to two years. They were expected to lend a hand wherever needed – visitation, sweeping, scrubbing, collecting mentally-handicapped children for the weekly special care unit, helping at the youth club, supporting our work with vagrant teenagers and drug abusers, and generally sharing the activities of a busy Salvation Army centre.

Almost from the inception of the scheme we had more applicants than we could take – from all sorts of young people. Most of them were Salvationists; some were members of other churches; a few were Christians with no particular denominational allegiance; one or two were agnostics. The reasons they gave for desiring to join us were invariably the same. They wanted to do something useful, to help to meet the need of under-privileged individuals.

The suitability of the applicants was not determined by their Christian profession only. Occasionally we preferred the agnostic youngster, a decision we took initially with reluctance and not a few misgivings, but one we never had reason to regret. We paid the young people a basic allowance of £5 a week plus accommodation and travelling expenses. They were expected to cater for themselves, both paying for and preparing their own meals. Five

or six young people were with us at any one time. They all worked
long hours on six days a week. The other day was a rest day
when significantly most of them slept until late morning or the
early hours of the afternoon. Without exception they were the
very spirit of service. Nothing was too demanding or too much
trouble. Sometimes, it's true, they preferred dramatic sacrifice to
the discipline of routine drudgery, but this neither surprised nor
disturbed us. They still applied themselves to the drudgery with
great zest and little oversight.

What did surprise us – and at first disturb us – was their
theology; to say that in some cases it was unorthodox is a gener-
ous understatement. Some of the young people appeared to have
rejected not only our every conceptualization of God, but God
himself. At first, I interpreted this as youthful arrogance and ignorance – theological ignorance, that is – but not for long. I discovered that the new thinking was expressed most convincingly
by the most thoughtful. The young people, some of them gradu-
ates, had rejected traditional concepts only after unhurried examination. They had read, argued, scrutinized their own spiritual
experience, talked to innumerable people for whom the traditional was still meaningful, and sought in every possible way to
understand precisely what their spiritual forebears believed and
why. They were not dogmatic, readily conceding that what in
major part was unacceptable to them was clearly effectual in the
lives of other believers. But they insisted that, for them, the
Christian faith in its present form was not intelligible or necessary.

They remained in the church, usually as members of the Salvation Army, because they had nowhere else to go. Our worship was
meaningless to them; they were bored by the singing and mystified by the public praying; open-air meetings, which they were
expected to support, seemed a waste of time and little more than
therapeutic for the participants; the whole weary routine of
customary activity was irrelevant to the point of fostering little
but a spirit of futility and near despair. But they believed in the
Salvation Army's social work if not its theology; and their whole
background and spiritual heritage, their families and friendships,
were centred in the Salvation Army. They *felt* they belonged,
though their minds rebelled. What should be done with them?
Dismiss them as heretics? Tell them not to wear Salvation Army

uniform? Insist that if they were not orthodox believers they were not Christians at all? Invite them to stop thinking for the sake of their own spiritual well-being?

Without wishing to minimize the importance of theology, of doctrines and creed, I wonder about priorities that put dogmas before devotion, and make conformity more essential than compassion. The young people I have in mind were not shouting their protest either to attract attention to themselves or to evade the moral challenge of Christian orthodoxy. They were already sacrificially involved in Christian caring, an example to all of us, even the most committed. If, as Jesus said, 'by their fruits ye shall know them', then these youngsters, unorthodox and unbelieving, heretical and rebellious, were essentially of his company, for they lived in his spirit and were committed to build a world in harmony with his teaching.

Within weeks of joining us, however, some of them were compelled to face a personal crisis of faith, one long evaded. The basic reasons were twofold. In the first place our vocabulary was largely meaningless to them. They were, of course, familiar with it, but the words we used, though obviously representing something real to us, evoked no response within their minds or emotions. We talked about God; they said that the word communicated nothing. We referred to the living Christ; they said that they knew the Jesus of history, the character portrayed in the four gospels, which they read assiduously, but the idea that this person was in some mystical way alive and able to share every moment of every day with them was to them empty of meaning. They did not doubt the reality of such an experience for me, and the multitudes of Salvationists like me, but they courteously insisted that such a statement of faith – and of course it could be no more – was not on their wavelength.

The second reason, a natural corollary of the first, accentuated the crisis. They had a religious faith – admittedly hazy and pulsating with more questions than answers – but no means of communicating it to the young people amongst whom they worked. At first, being uniform-wearing Salvationists, they felt committed to paying lip-service to conventional doctrines and the sort of biblical phrases they knew so well, but increasingly they became uneasy about it. For not only did they lack personal conviction, but their young listeners, like my schoolboys, the members of our youth club and the flower children, had no time and less inclination for their Christian propaganda.

Now it seemed to me that their faith in God was as real as mine. But, as I have said, they did not talk about God. The very name, they explained, represented little more than pointers in the general direction of truth. When people talked about God they were referring to their limited and probably distorted understanding of him. The concept and the reality were utterly different. So argued my young colleagues. But this was not their usual approach or interest. They preferred to exchange ideas about how to *live* rather than what to *believe*, particularly when the latter seemed to them to be little more than theological hair-splitting. Their outlook and the conundrum they represented can perhaps best be focused by a quotation from the Archbishop of Canterbury's book, *God, Christ and the World*. Commenting critically on a central theme from Harvey Cox's *The Secular City*, the Archbishop wrote:

> The truth of God's transcendence still stands. God is near, but God is different. God is here, but man is dependent. God's otherness is the otherness of Creator to creature, of Saviour to sinner; and it is for the creature still to worship the Creator and for the sinner still to ask for the Saviour's grace. Without this the new Christianity of the secular city will lose its identity as Christianity and will deceive itself and mislead its citizens. And, on the other hand, those who cherish God's transcendence will know that it is within the secular city that it has to be vindicated and that the transcendent and the numinous are to be seen not in a separate realm of religious practice but in human lives marked by an awe-inspiring self-forgetfulness, compassion, humility and courage. Such lives bear witness that we have here no continuing city, for we are looking for a city which is to come.[1]

This is well said and, I believe, makes a necessary emphasis. But what happens when 'awe-inspiring self-forgetfulness, compassion, humility and courage' are seen – seen clearly and consistently – in the lives of individuals indifferent to the transcendent or at least its customary definitions? The young people I have in mind did bear witness that 'we have here no continuing city', but this was not their conscious aim or motivation. They were compassionate simply because they believed that people mattered

[1] SCM Press 1969, p.29f.

for no other reason than that they were people. There was no deliberate attempt to be compassionate, to do the compassionate thing. They loved others, not because they loved God, but because they believed that loving relationships were mutually fulfilling and alone gave meaning to life. They cared and served in a spirit free of self-conscious virtue. The explanation was not their faith in transcendent Being, but their faith in people, including many social and moral cripples often totally ignored by devout orthodox believers.

The last thing I want to do is to invent a false dichotomy between thinking and living or belief and behaviour, as though the two are not related and expressions of each other. Equally, I have no desire to suggest that belief is unimportant, even by comparison with practical living, or that theological and philosophical considerations get in the way of life's real issues. But I am concerned about emphases and priorities. I wonder about God being known only when consciously and correctly identified in conventional theological terms. Is he so restricted by finite man's definitions? And is not his revelation ongoing and, like his word, capable of more light and new manifestations? All I know is that a growing number of young people rejected my theology, but wanted to share my work. They dedicated themselves to build a kingdom of right relationships, which is surely what Jesus meant when he talked about the kingdom of God. Despite their indifference to the traditional means of grace which I found indispensable, they exemplified many of the fruits of the Spirit. I worshipped God in public and in private, which means from a practical standpoint that I sought to give worth-ship to those things that harmonize with the mind of God as revealed by Jesus. My young friends, without deliberate worship of God or any other sort of conscious transcendental relationship, also gave worth-ship to the same values and loyalties, but for reasons simply of their veneration of human personality. Yet they were far more than humanists or secularists. Their whole lives reflected the outlook of the Man for others.

They typify, I believe, multitudes of British young people. Organizations like Voluntary Service Overseas have revealed that they receive far more applications than they can place, and that the majority of them are from individuals not motivated by conscious Christian conviction. They offer because, having assessed in a matter-of-fact way the plight of needy people, they want to help, to make a contribution to meet that need. They are the first to admit the influence of other factors behind their applications – the call of adventure, the wish to travel, the longing for change – but this does not alter the fact that their basic desire is to alleviate human suffering. Some of them have records of service that in terms of dedication and sacrifice add chapters to the Acts of the Apostles, but they operate outside the structures of institutional religion and apparently feel no need for the ministry of the church. Are we therefore to conclude that God is outside their experience? Or could it be that they know God by some other name? I realize, of course, that these questions are not new, but they have never been answered positively. The church is sometimes the incarnation of ambiguity; we Christians do tend to come down heavily on both sides – just in case. We say not yes or no, but amen. I am convinced that hordes of young people will be lost to the church unless we face the challenge of their secular Christian living. It is not yet too late, but time is running out. A growing number of them, having despaired of the church, see themselves as taking her place in the vanguard of social reform. They are deeply involved whenever the great moral and social issues are being debated, and their development is more than academic. They believe in action, sometimes called non-violent protest or rebellion according to your point of view. But, significantly, they are always on the side of the underdog, the little man who is often incapable of helping himself. They accuse the church of having big convictions about little things, and little convictions about big things. No one denies that their judgment is often extreme, based on too little evidence and more a protest than a constructive policy, but, unlike many of their critics, they are living at the centre of life and wrestling with the things that concern the dignity of *every* man. My main purpose in writing like this is not to eulogize modern youth, though to do so might help to counterbalance the disproportionate influence of a vocal minority in their number, a grossly unrepresentative group whose aptitude for publicity is in inverse ratio to their real newsworthiness. My purpose is to claim and to illustrate that God, the Spirit of love and truth, is the inspiration behind the moral and social crusades of young people today.

And indeed not only of *young* people. More and more individuals of all ages are unconsciously fashioning their lives upon the ultimate concerns of Christianity. They are doing this outside the church, with two significant results. There are, I believe, more Christians outside than inside the church; and there is more Christianity in Britain today than ever before. Such assertions will infuriate some Christians and most humanists for diametrically opposite reasons. The former will point to the permissive society with its superficial symptoms of irresponsible living, and insist that moral fruits require spiritual roots. The latter will claim that I want the best of both worlds at the expense of truth – their truth. I see the persuasiveness of both points of view, and will return to such considerations in Chapter Six, but first I want to look at another aspect of evangelism altogether – the question of our motivation.

# 4

# *People before Converts*

We were increasingly involved. The gulf that normally existed between ourselves and pagan youth was bridged, at least physically and I think socially; we were accepted. But for the rest we were getting nowhere, or so we feared. I had a gospel, proved over the years in personal experience, but found myself no more intelligible in trying to communicate it than a man using sign language to the uninitiated; and my young colleagues, like a number of others associated with us, people of widely different ages and backgrounds, had a faith that represented more the rejection of traditional Christianity and institutional religion than articulated belief.

The last thing I want to do is to give the impression that their rejection was unconditional. This explains, of course, the ambiguity of the whole situation. But it was sufficiently extensive and significant to create real problems, particularly in terms of how to communicate the faith. Which leads naturally to the question of *their* faith. Did they have any? And if so what was its object and dynamic? The surprising thing was that they themselves found such questions unnecessary. They argued that life was to be lived, not analysed into neat verbal definitions of theology. However, they were clearly more than humanists, far, far more. For their whole way of life reflected the spiritual perspective that Jesus Christ taught; and that word *perspective* is, I think, important. The secularist is one-dimensional in his thinking and living. He sees everything primarily in strictly materialistic and temporal terms. For him concepts like spiritual and eternal, soul and supernatural, God and theistic communion, are not only unnecessary; they are dangerous as diversions from reality. He prides himself in having shaken free from the myths and biblical fairy tales which once enslaved gullible mankind. Such concessions to human immaturity are no longer desirable. Man has come of age and is capable of managing without reference to the spiritual crutches of his former crippled existence.

The Christian agnostics associated with me were of an entirely different outlook. They believed in the spiritual dimension; indeed, without it they believed that much of life's glory was reduced to meaningless baubles and crude biological impulses. But believing in this perspective and articulating it to young sceptics were hardly the same exercise. The former did not inspire the latter. Meanwhile, we were all inescapably involved with people of widely different temperaments and characters.

About one thing we were unanimous, and this represented a revolution in my thinking rather than theirs. We should stop thinking of evangelism as a means of inflating our congregations. Since the days of which I am writing, a lot of troubled water has flowed under the bridge of evangelical debate, and now most of us are agreed that to treat people as pew fodder, and little else, is, considerations of effectiveness apart, a denial of everything central to Christianity. But it took a long time for some of us to perceive this elementary truth, and even now I come across frightening evidence that some Christian zealots are motivated in all their evangelical outreach by one obsession only – to fill pews and get people converted. On the surface, of course, nothing could seem more reasonable. People need the gospel. They are frustrated, ridden with guilt, plagued by anxiety, living at cross-purposes with themselves and God. He has the answer to their plight, an answer he revealed in Jesus Christ and committed to his church. Logically if conversion is what people need, then the church's preoccupation should be evangelism, getting people converted. What could be more natural, therefore, than that pew-filling should have top priority in the aims of all loyal churchmen, not to mention keen evangelicals. As I say, on the surface the argument makes sense. But beneath the surface it represents nothing less than devout blasphemy, a spirit that has done more harm to the cause of Christ's kingdom than multitudes of non-church-goers. It is devout because its sincere aim is to serve God and further his cause. But it is blasphemy because it uses God's name to manipulate and condition other people. Perhaps the issue can be brought into sharper focus if we look at a number of real situations, all of them known to myself.

The first one concerns old people. A few years ago the Salvation Army launched a nation-wide scheme to establish 'over-sixty' clubs. The need for such weekly gatherings, and the programme of social service that flowed out of them, was urgent. Many pensioners were lonely and bored. With time on their hands and nowhere to go, they gravitated, especially the men, to library reading rooms, betting shops, cafés and coffee bars; the women, with their fellowship meetings and sewing circles, were better placed, but many of them remained isolated and friendless. The Salvation Army's immediate aim was characteristically down-to-earth – it was simply to provide the opportunity for a weekly get-together, a time for games, singing, talking and tea-drinking, not forgetting the inevitable formal religion at the end. Clubs sprang up all over the country and soon in some cities and towns were a major activity. This development was not, however, universally popular with Salvation Army officers. Some of them argued that it represented yet another unfortunate diversion from their main task of evangelism. Others justified the vast expenditure of strength, time and money involved in running the clubs with the comforting thought that converts might result. One fiery evangelist, sincere, dedicated and industrious, summed up the attitude of a small minority when he refused to establish a club on the grounds that God had called him to build an army, not act as nursemaid to people with one foot in the grave. He was not callous or insensitive. His friends described him as a man with a 'passion for souls'. He was single-minded in seeking to fulfil his vocation, particularly in organizing events to fill his pews. But he turned from a ministry to human need in the name of building first the kingdom of God. He put converts before people. He thought more of saving souls than serving sinners.

The basic trouble was that, like the evangelical zealots who still think like him, he was not committed to people for their own intrinsic value. He was committed to them as a means to an end; the end was laudable enough, but when it made the means little more than an exercise in pious self-interest, there was something drastically wrong.

I remember being invited to a youth club to conduct what was erroneously called the epilogue. When I arrived the place was a hive of happiness. There were youngsters everywhere, singing, laughing, jiving, drinking pepsi, playing table games, boys chatting up girls, and some club workers talking with easy informality to club members, no small achievement in itself. Not for a long time, if ever before, had I come across such a spirit of club gaiety. It was infectious and stimulating. Suddenly everything stopped. The record-player was switched off, the canteen closed, the games were halted, the laughter and singing subsided, and the doors were locked. It was time for the epilogue, half-way through the evening!

One of the workers whispered in my ear that this was the only way to guarantee maximum attendance. The rule was simple and to the point. If you missed the epilogue you were locked out for the remainder of the night. No religion, no more fun in the second half. You either stayed or stayed out. Within seconds that club was transformed into a quiet, cold, hostile assembly. The music stopped; the gaiety evaporated; and the reason – religion or, as another worker explained to me, the evangelical purpose behind the club's existence. Mentally I crawled to the centre of the floor to officiate. I felt embarrassed, humiliated and ashamed. Whatever I said was blatantly contradicted by the situation itself, and the youngsters' attitude of polite defiance indicated that this point had not passed them by. Within seconds of the epilogue ending, the club came back to life. The members were once more free to enjoy themselves. They had paid the price for their fun by suffering the epilogue; and with the firm impression that religion was a kill-joy that stopped singing and laughter and music and everything else that made for real living they gratefully returned to their 'irreligious' ways. Seven years later I happened to pass those club premises again. They were closed and derelict. But doubtless the so-called evangelicals responsible for this inevitable outcome were elsewhere preaching the word, foisting upon other resentful minds a damaging and damnable interpretation of the gospel; the gospel which, above everything else, insists that every individual, being unique and precious in the sight of God, should be treated with profound respect and never as a pawn in an evangelical game. What obscures the essential issue in all this – and the two illustrations I have given are cases in point – is that the people concerned are not bad or unscrupulous, the very opposite. They love God, say their prayers, and read their Bible. They have integrity and sincerity. Their aim is to serve God and win converts to his cause. Despite their sometimes unconscious use of moral blackmail and spiritual bullying, threats of hellfire and all that, they are themselves usually gentle and tolerant. But all too often their only interest in people is spiritual or evangelical. They make relationships not with individuals but with potential converts. They minister, often at great personal sacrifice, not to meet physical need, but as a means of using physical need to save souls. There is a subtle difference and a vital one. It points to the reason why Christian caring is sometimes little more than an evangelical tactic. It explains why all too frequently Christian caring is initiated and sustained only when it promises results in organizational advancement and conversions. A certain type of evangelical soon loses heart and interest in any project that does not immediately lend itself to formal preaching or early justify itself in the number of converts registered. Obviously I am not referring to all evangelicals; the ones I have in mind are not even typical. But they do exist, and their attitude is, I believe, seriously hindering the whole church in its compassionate ministry, a ministry motivated by concern free of self-aggrandizement and self-centredness.

I write with authority, for, until the moment of truth dawned for me, I was at least tainted by this spirit of misguided zeal. My single-minded concern was to win converts. It still is. But converts or not, I see now that people are important and significant and of infinite value for themselves alone. That one insight – it seems so elementary now – revolutionized my approach to people and compelled me to see them with new eyes. It also made possible my happy partnership with Christians who did not share my theological position and with non-Christians whose compassion, expressed in costly involvement with the needy, was a further stimulant to furious theological debate.

# 5

# *The Torments of Involvement*

Apart from our unanimity about the importance of seeing people as infinitely more than merely potential pew fodder, we were agreed without reservation about one or two related matters. For instance, we determined to identify ourselves as completely as possible with the people to whom we sought to minister. If that word *minister* has unfortunate associations of sanctimonious patronage, I am sorry, but unrepentant about its use. We wanted to minister. It seemed to us that this was what life was all about. We knew how easy it was to serve without the spirit of service, to give and thereby cheapen the recipient, to do good and be little more than well-meaning do-gooders. For too long we had thought in terms of them and us, of converted and unconverted, of saints and sinners. Now we wanted, above all, to create relationships of mutual respect and confidence, to destroy barriers of suspicion and distrust. For years some of us had been engaged in so-called militant evangelism, shouting our message from the centre of a street during an open-air meeting, challenging strangers on their doorsteps and seeing them again, if at all, only during our next brief evangelical sortie in their neighbourhood. We called such exercises hand-to-hand combat or, more ludicrous still, *personal* contacting, for the whole approach was guaranteed to confirm and strengthen its impersonal nature. People were faces and not personalities. We did not know them or give them the opportunity to get to know us. We were strangers talking to strangers about something they did not want to hear about. There was no involvement, no real encounter. The basic trouble was, of course, that we were not identified with the people where they were; and our only answer apparently was to shout at them to come over and join us.

To be identified with people in their need – their sometimes unpleasant, bewildering and unrealized need – is never easy and, once experienced, is only sustained if prompted by authentic caring. This principle of identification obviously applies in every stratum of society in which the evangelist is operating: no, not operating, just living. But its costly implications are seen more vividly in those segments of society where physical and material need is rampant and often gruesome. In his book *Come Out the Wilderness*, Bruce Kenrick had this to say about Christian involvement in the slums of East Harlem:

Identification would mean living in the same kind of apartment and amid the same garbage as others in East Harlem. It would mean taking their families along, and exposing their children to the same temptations as the children who lived next door. It would mean being always at the disposal of the people with whom they sought identity, always having an open door, always responding to a visitor's knock, however late in the night it might come; it would mean, in other words, an abandonment of privacy and a free welcome into their family circle for the drug addict and the drunks and the friendless and the thieves. Identification with East Harlem would mean looking down the dismal streets and saying, 'This is my home; this is where I belong'. [1]

We were concerned in our immediate situation about young drifters, drug abusers and similar social rejects, sometimes called drop-outs, but more correctly push-outs, the victims of society's rat-race mentality and obsession with material success. Their way of life, whichever way you looked at it, was hardly conducive to comfort. Yet to reach them we knew that we had to be identified with them. Stated like that, the impression might be given that our identification was to be little more than part of a new evangelical technique with the same old ulterior motivation; and of course such unconscious scheming was always possible. But we knew that without realistic identification we would never be accepted, and without acceptance there could be no chance of creative personal relationships.

However, this identification created other problems. Once evangelical Christians get involved with characters of dubious reputation and worse, they leave themselves wide open to charges

[1] Collins 1963; Fontana edition, p. 3.

of at least impropriety. I recall the story of Vatalis, a Christian hermit of some sixty years of age who lived in the seventh century. Meditating one day in the lonely Gaza desert, he read the story of the woman taken in adultery. As he prayed he heard a voice: 'Vatalis, what are you doing here?' The hermit fell to his knees, convinced that the questioner was God. 'You know why I am here,' he replied, not without indignation, 'I am meditating upon your word, seeking further understanding.' The heavenly voice was insistent, 'What are you doing here, Vatalis?' The monk was too exasperated to reply. 'You should be at Alexandria where many women like the one of whom you have just read await news of the gospel.'

The old man – he was very old for his times – hurriedly packed his few belongings and set out for the city. Immediately on arrival, despite his weariness, he made for certain streets and visited from house to house, telling the women who would listen of God's love and forgiveness. Sometimes in his zeal he went inside. If the women's interest justified it, he remained with them all night and was often successful in persuading them to leave their life of shame.

His greatest critics were, of course, members of the local church. Far from merely raising their eyebrows, they suggested, first behind raised hands and then openly, that he was up to no good. All those nights of prayer! They knew the real reason behind his nocturnal devotions. He was, they said, a disgrace to the gospel and bringing the whole Christian community into disrepute. How could their witness be effective when such a man was corrupting their influence? They attacked him at every opportunity, separated themselves from him, and prayed that God would open his eyes to the truth. Meanwhile, one of their number, not unmindful that though the mills of God work slow they grind exceeding sure, decided nevertheless to push things on a bit. He concealed himself outside a house of shame, and when the little monk emerged from his errand of mercy attacked and killed him. At the funeral many of the women, now redeemed and themselves humble followers of Christ, walked in tribute behind the coffin and testified that through Vatalis's simple goodness they had been led to a new way of life. Soon members of the local church shared in the general lamentation, deploring the martyrdom and glorying in the virtues of the martyr. At the appropriate time Vatalis was canonized, and his tomb of shame turned into a shrine.

Yes, realistic identification does have its problems; and the final outcome is not always so pleasant. Unconventional goodness that puts people before principle, and love before law usually leads to a cross of some sort. Jesus himself was condemned for the company he kept. His critics sneeringly described him as the 'friend of publicans and sinners', of quislings and harlots, as though that in itself was enough to prove their accusations against him of compromise and corruption. Would a holy man, they inferred, have such friends and visit such places of revelry?

Men of devout habits continue to talk of the need to 'shun every appearance of evil', and, with the same imagined biblical authority, exhort believers to 'come out from among them and be separate'; *them* being, of course, sinners, people of the world. Apparently, they never look at the biblical context. If they did they would see that by *them* the apostle was referring to notorious sinners within the church, individuals who, despite their continued profession of faith, practised open immorality. It was these people from whom sincere believers were to separate themselves. The apostle was explicit about this. In correcting an obvious misunderstanding of his words in a previous letter he explained that if he had been exhorting Christians to separate themselves from people of the world he would have been asking them to contract out of society altogether, and this clearly had not been his intention. Nevertheless, among evangelicals today this same old controversy still rages. To be or not to be separated from the world, that is the question. I only mention it because it is related to this vital matter of identification. But let me make my own position abundantly clear. I believe that separation as taught by some evangelicals is wrong in principle and disastrous in practice; that it represents one of the worst forms of spiritual snobbery and the final triumph of Pharisaism; and that, being the extreme opposite of the spirit of Jesus, it breeds those sins of the spirit which, though most obnoxious, are made doubly insidious by their pose as fruits of righteousness. It is not so long ago that some evangelicals measured personal holiness in terms of not going to cinemas and theatres, not wearing worldly dress, and not buying ice cream or newspapers on Sundays. We shall see how the thinking behind such abstentions, though not necessarily the abstentions themselves, has encouraged the letter to defeat the spirit of the law, and often turned sour even the milk of human kindness. For the moment I want to return to this question of identification and the inescapable involvement that goes with it.

Once an evangelical, out of genuine compassion, identifies himself with people who do not share his moral susceptibilities, he finds himself facing all manner of moral dilemmas. He does not judge, and has no wish to do so. Less still does he condemn. Other considerations apart, he knows that such an approach only alienates, if not antagonizes. Yet to witness open and repeated defiance of moral law – pilfering, sexual promiscuity, deceit and much else – and not categorically to condemn it is surely to appear to condone it. Indeed, is it possible in such circumstances not to condemn without condoning? In seeking an answer, or even a little more light, we must avoid the danger of over-simplification; the very complexity of the situation explains why some evangelicals play safe and indulge in wholesale condemnation. Far better, they argue, to let people know where you stand than to win false popularity at the price of guilty silence. They have a point, but unfortunately one not related to the matter under discussion; and their attitude creates an uneasy suspicion that they are more concerned about safeguarding their reputation than helping the people they are condemning.

Perhaps we shall best see some of the thorny problems in clearer outline by considering a true-life situation. When Father Borrelli, a young Roman Catholic priest, wanted to help the homeless boys of Naples, he faced two major obstacles. In the first place, he had to receive permission from his superiors for the work to be initiated, and they were adamant in their refusal. His intentions, they agreed, were excellent; and certainly something should be done to remedy what amounted to a national scandal. But for the church to get involved in an area of human need bristling with so many difficulties was foolhardy. Borrelli continued over many months to plead for ecclesiastical consent, but always the answer was the same – return to your parish and be a faithful priest there. He did, with the gentleness of a dove. Happily he was also learning to be as wise as a serpent, surprisingly so for one so unpractised in church diplomacy. He explained to his spiritual peers that the

Salvation Army was now seeking to provide for the homeless boys
and would, unless the church moved quickly to do likewise, undoubtedly receive increasing publicity, publicity that would both
indict the church and benefit the Salvation Army. Permission was
immediately granted.

The second barrier was seemingly insurmountable. The boys
themselves hated authorities in general and priests in particular.
Borrelli quickly perceived that the only way to overcome this
endemic hatred was to become one of the gang himself; to identify
himself with the boys so completely that, until he decided otherwise, they would never suspect that he was a priest. Fortunately
his boyish face and slight body enabled him without difficulty
to look like one of the boys, but to be accepted by them was
another matter altogether. To achieve this, he knew that he would
have to live with them and give not the slightest indication that
he did not share their normally amoral way of life. They lied,
pilfered, worked as pimps for prostitutes, exploited every situation possible for self-gain, and in numerous other ways were
compelled to evade the law. Borrelli lived like them. He had to.
That was what realistic identification was all about for him.
And after some twelve months he was sufficiently confident of
the boys' friendship and acceptance to reveal his true identity.
One of the leaders spat in his face and walked away. But the vast
majority, after a few incredulous moments, agreed to accompany
him to what proved to be the first of a growing number of Borrelli
homes. To read the remarkable story in detail is to enter a new
dimension of Christian caring; to be moved to laughter and tears,
to praise and penitence. But the questions remain. Was Borrelli
right? Did the end justify the means? Is it possible to be morally
wrong, but spiritually right? To what extent, if any, does love
supersede law? In pondering such questions we need constantly
to remind ourselves that we are not indulging in either theological
hair-splitting or academic exercises in situation ethics. Father
Borrelli was a real person facing real people in a real setting. What
was he to do? And does he in retrospect still think that his approach
was right? Morris West, his biographer, was mercilessly probing
in seeking to find out:

'You are a priest, Don Borrelli. How did you square your conscience
with your actions as a *scugnizzo*?' He looked at me sharply. He had been

interviewed by many people, but I was the first, I think, who had probed so close to the core of the matter. It was a long time before he replied. When his answer came, it was pieced out with meticulous care, as if he were trying to explain it, not only to me but to himself.

'It was my endeavour, so far as possible, to withdraw myself from the direct act of sin. For instance I never stole, personally. I never solicited directly for a girl. I participated, certainly, in the act, but I tried so far as possible to make my participation a matter of appearance, to withdraw it, as much as I could, from the substance of the act.'

'But in fact you did participate?'

'Yes.'

'And did share in the fruits of the act?'

'Yes.'

'Was that justifiable in law and conscience?'

Borrelli pushed a tired hand through his hair and looked at me steadily. I was ashamed of my insistence but, if I were to arrive at the truth of the man, I must have the answer. He gave it to me, quietly.

'Much of it was justifiable, yes. Much of it was, shall we say, on the razor edge between right and wrong. But I was committed, you see. I could not turn back. I could only make my own judgment and commit it to the mercy of God. Even so ...'

He broke off and looked down at the palms of his work-man's hands.

'Even so?'

'Even so,' said Don Borrelli, softly, 'there were many moments when I was a *scugnizzo* and not a priest.'[1]

There are no easy answers, which is why some of us escape the dilemmas by evading the identification, the too costly involvement. Jesus, of course, never did. We have seen that, in consequence, he was accused of ignoring one of the imagined essentials of personal sanctity – separation from sinners and their haunts – but significantly he continued freely to associate with individuals normally ostracized by the devout. Surely, one of the intimations of his greatness was his ability to create, with all sorts of people, relationships devoid of embarrassment and painful self-consciousness. Ordinary individuals, let alone notorious sinners, are not usually noted for their desire to fraternize with religious teachers and the like. Ask any dog-collar-wearing train traveller! But Jesus, holiest of men, mixed freely with misfits and rejects of society who clearly enjoyed his company. They felt neither rejected nor condemned by him. The four gospels suggest that though

[1] Morris West, *Children of the Sun*, Heinemann 1957; Pan Books edition, pp. 91-2.

sometimes he had scathing words to say to the Pharisees and
other professional religionists, he never condemned 'publicans
and sinners'. It was not that he approved of their ways or was
more tolerant of their sins of the flesh as distinct from the Pharisees' sins of the spirit. He was simply saying in deeds what
psychologists started to shout 1900 years later, that to condemn
a man who is already down and struggling with feelings of
inferiority, insignificance and failure is to deepen his sense of
rejection and further to undermine his self-respect. His natural
reaction is to retaliate, to reject as he is rejected, an attitude
hardly conducive to happy relationships with his condemners.
Yet, in my experience, we evangelicals, with our puritan con-
sciences, tend quickly to judge and condemn individuals whose
way of life falls beneath certain moral standards and social con-
ventions. We appear to see every long-haired youngster as a
potential layabout; and our attitude to drug addicts, hippies we
don't understand, spirit drinkers, and other moral cripples is a
denial of the spirit in which Jesus lived among their counterparts
of his day. He took the risk of appearing to condone sinful ways.
He lost his reputation for righteousness. As the apostle Paul later
wrote in another connection. 'He made himself of no reputation';
and there are few things more difficult to surrender even to God
than a reputation for goodness.

The remarkable thing was that though he refused to condemn
'publicans and sinners', they had no illusions about his attitude
to their sins. Being the kind of people they were, they would have
been the first to have despised him for the slightest evidence of
moral laxity on his part, and to have shouted their charges of
hypocrisy from the housetops. Each of the four gospels indicates,
however, that whatever the *separatists* said about the meaning of
his free association with 'sinners', the sinners themselves never
doubted his uncompromising personal goodness. They knew
where he stood, respected him for it, and realized well enough
what he thought of their sinful ways. What he *was* communicated itself with pungent inoffensiveness; yes, inoffensiveness.
For what is the use of making anyone feel more rejected, guilty,
depressed, unwanted, and inadequate? I doubt whether Jesus ever
talked to groups of sinners about their sins. The subject was too
personal and private for general public discussion. And the few

private conversations recorded in the gospels suggest that Jesus rarely talked to individuals about their sins at all; and never before, as with Zacchaeus, the initiative had come from them. It seems to me that evangelical moralists, apart from unconsciously revealing the poverty of their own religious faith, adopt tactics that are inescapably self-defeating. Christianity has to be caught, not taught; imbibed, not imposed. It rubs off on people as they are brought into closer association with its authentic spirit. If it doesn't, better to keep quiet anyway.

This explains why Jesus, despite his free involvement with people normally shunned in the name of religion and public morality, never gave them the wrong impression. They knew that he did not condone; words were unnecessary. They saw the truth in his eyes, felt the gentle rebuke of his spirit, and longed to be like him. But this was because first they *enjoyed* his company. He was not a preacher, but a friend; one of them, approachable, understanding, human, good for a laugh, alive. He wasn't trying to do them good or scheming to make contact with them for the sake of propagating his faith. He loved them. He accepted them unconditionally, just as they were, with their sins and irreverence, their feelings of insecurity and inadequacy. Neither did he make demands beyond their moral capacity nor lecture them about moral standards beyond their own desires. He loved them for themselves. Far from being censorious towards them, he lived among them in a spirit of compassion and forgiveness, the forgiveness that takes the initiative in seeking to heal broken relationships. Not that his attitude was conscious or a pose, a crafty technique to win converts; it was the spontaneous expression of true love's profound insight. He saw beneath the surface upon which most of us live to the essential man or woman whose sins and anti-social ways were really a cry for help. Without sentiment, he believed that evil appearances were often the ploys behind which frightened souls sought refuge from the fierce demands of society, a society loud in its protestations of faith in God but guilty of practical atheism. With the patience that is free to wait with purpose, he relentlessly pursued the real man or woman, cutting through foibles and personal idiosyncrasies until the true self was recognized and made aware of its own God-given potential.

Jesus was so at one with God himself that he was free to live in a spirit of forgiveness; and forgiveness, above all, restores broken relationships. We have already insisted that without relationships of mutual respect, trust and acceptance, evangelical activity, whatever its nature, is nothing more than an exercise in self-centred piety. Yet how often evangelicals, fearful of getting too mixed-up with undesirable elements, rush in, make their verbal witness, not infrequently with threats of judgment to come, and gratefully withdraw to their fellowships of like-minded believers. Meanwhile, the world passes them by, with resentment, amusement, or indifference. And it will continue to do so until, leaving their bastions of puritanism, and risking their reputations for uncompromising righteousness, they share their Master's identification with 'publicans and sinners', share it with his compassion and perception, and in a spirit utterly free of ulterior motivation and censoriousness.

# 6

# *God is Astonished Joy*

It seems to me that our social history alone proves my point that there is more Christianity in Britain today than ever before. Never have we as a nation been more concerned about every individual. Social legislation has centred on guaranteeing a square deal for everybody. We have a long way to go, but progress over the past fifty years represents, I claim, not only a herculean attempt to meet physical and material need, but the recognition that other vital factors are involved in ministering to total human personality. Not so long ago, as some of our fathers and grandfathers can remember, deprived members of the community were treated as less than human. They worked, if they could get a job at all, for long hours and little pay. Children sometimes walked a labour treadmill for a pittance. There were either no pensions, unemployment grants, sick benefits, and other allowances now taken for granted, or the amounts were insulting and humiliating. The workhouse was as much needed as it was feared. But attitudes have changed. Certain types of people are no longer looked upon as inferior and undeserving of *charity*, now a dirty word. The life of the whole nation is more compassionate. There is greater understanding of human need, deeper insight into human personality, and better opportunities for the vast majority of people to find personal fulfilment. Most people are outraged at social injustice and care about basic human rights. As a nation we are anxious to make better provision for the aged, the sick, the homeless. I repeat, we have a long way to go; but I still believe that the spirit of the total community is more in harmony with the aims of Christianity than ever before.

That brings me to my first proposition – that there are more Christians outside than inside the church. Of course this immedi-

ately poses such questions as what is the church and what or who is
a Christian? We could doubtless have a lively discussion with such
themes, and get nowhere. Our more direct concern is with
Christian living, a major emphasis of the New Testament. Is
there anywhere in the four gospels the slightest indication that
orthodoxy of belief is essential to Christian living? Or have the
saints – even the few we have known personally – been strictly
conventional in their views, let alone their beliefs? Looking at
the world church, we might well ask what is orthodoxy of belief
anyway but, that apart, can we justifiably assume, both from
history and our own observations, that Christian living is not
dependent upon orthodox belief or indeed upon conscious belief
in God at all? Throughout my life I have known numerous people
who, indifferent to institutional religion in every way, have nevertheless revealed qualities of Christlikeness. As I continue to
associate freely with all sorts of individuals outside the church
I am impressed by the amount of heroic goodness and genuine
unselfishness that I find. In that sense only do I mean that there
are more Christians outside the church than inside. Then what is
the difference, if any, between such Christians and people equally
good who call themselves humanists? Probably nothing at all from
a fundamental standpoint; but let me try to explain in more detail
what I mean. Whenever I talk to people I call Christians outside
the church I find invariably that when pressed to analyse their
philosophy or faith they confess belief in many of the things that
Christ emphasized as being crucial to personal fulfilment and
creative personal relationships. They subscribe to his ideals and
work for their implementation in every department of life.
Unknown to themselves, they *do* 'bear witness that we have here
no continuing city', for the very spirit in which they live points
to a reality beyond itself.

Now whatever our theological position, we are probably agreed
that the life of Jesus was characterized by three great attributes:
his sense of *awe*; his attitude of selfless *love*; and his awareness of
*ultimate accountability*. His awe was engendered in the presence
of God, using that word as most orthodox Christians understand
it, but surely not only so. He must also have been gripped by awe
in the presence of life's mysteries – its love and laughter, its
suffering and sorrow, its blessing and bewilderment. It can be

rightly argued that the awe with which Jesus approached the whole of life originated in and was deepened by his consciousness of God's nearness, but such a spirit – the spirit of wonder, of astonished joy – is related to many so-called secular experiences in life. Who has not been gripped by it in the presence of children? Ask any father how he felt when peering into the cot of his new-born child for the first time. He knew that he was on holy ground, confronted by mystery, the sort of mystery that leads to wonder, the wonderment that is akin to worship and veneration. This same awe grips us in the presence of beauty, courage, death, danger. On the very day I was writing this chapter, a letter arrived from a young Australian friend. He wrote:

A few weeks ago we had a powerful reminder to consider our priorities when we ran off the road, crashed down a 30-foot gully into a creek, wrote off our six-week-old car, and escaped with a few scratches, thanks to our being well strapped in ... all is well now and back to normal. But life is very fragile and we take risks every day. It seems cockeyed that so many of us go like mad for security in every aspect of our lives and then take appalling risks in the most trivial situations. Perhaps the order has to be reversed. To take big risks on big issues ...

The point is that near-death stopped him in his tracks in more ways than one. It compelled him to lift his mental eyes away from the immediate to consider his ultimate concerns; and those concerns were by other names the same truths and values to which Jesus bore witness. Self-evidently I am not arguing that awesomeness is related to conscious faith in God or awareness of his presence alone, but it is, I believe, related to that dimension of life which Jesus, by his life, death and resurrection, brought into sharpest focus and interpreted most comprehensively. In so far as we are capable of this awe, of experiencing what from another standpoint Albert Schweitzer called 'reverence for life', we are in touch with this dimension and living in the spirit of Jesus.

I remember reading *The Cult of Sincerity* in which the author, Herbert Read, testified that Martin Buber (who liked to call himself an anthropological philosopher) and Carl Jung (who liked to call himself a scientific psychologist) were 'the most persistent influence in the latter part of my own life'. He went on:

Buber believed in a personal relationship with 'the spirit of God', 'the image of God', whom he also called 'the Creator'. Man is completed, made whole, by exposure to 'the creative Spirit'. Jung was more ambiguous, but when asked whether he believed in God, answered, 'I do not believe: I know'. He knew, not so much from his own experience (as in Buber's case) but from his awareness of the spirit of God in other people, the people who came to him for healing, and whom he could not heal without God's help. I cannot bear witness to the presence of God, [continued Herbert Read] either in Buber's sense or in Jung's sense, and yet I am not a materialist. All my life I have found more sustenance in the work of those who bear witness to the reality of a living God than in the work of those who deny God.... In that state of suspense, 'waiting on God', I still live and shall probably die.[1]

In the light of Herbert Read's writings, notably some of his poems and his autobiography, I wonder whether by the time he died, in 1968, he was still waiting on God or had realized by then that he knew him by some other name. As he said, he was not a materialist, and everything about his life and thought suggests that he knew the Reality to which other more orthodox believers bear ready witness. His sense of awe in the face of life's imponderables was, I believe, the attitude of 'creature to Creator, of sinner to Saviour', and evidence that he was in touch with transcendent Being.

A symptom of crass materialism is the arrogance with which some secularists contrast science and emotion, as though to seek truth by means others than scientific is an open invitation to inescapable error. The scientific method, they assert, is free of emotion, being concerned only with facts, with objective reality. Fair enough. So it should be. But we are seeking, at this point, simply to illustrate that the secularist, with his materialistic obsession, is in danger – put it no stronger than that – of cutting himself off from an essential dimension of life of which the Christian asserts Jesus was and is the fullest finite manifestation. And if ever that dimension or spiritual interpretation disappears completely from his thinking and living – assuming that this is entirely possible – then, I believe, his capacity for awe will be destroyed at source. He will be truly a materialist. But surely we all see the difference between this man and the person who calls himself a materialist, lives with no conscious reference to God, and yet who subscribes in experience to many of the values that belong to the kingdom as revealed by Jesus. Of this I feel con-

[1] Faber & Faber 1969, p. 34.

fident – that one of the major differences between them will be their contrasting capacities for awe.

In an age of science and technology, when extreme technocrats tend to be too busy tinkering with their machines to waste time on spiritual profundities, it seems to me that what this world drugged by materialism urgently needs is the gift of wonder. William Wordsworth summed it up in words that begin with probably his best-known couplet:

> My heart leaps up when I behold
> A rainbow in the sky;
> So was it when my life began;
> So be it now I am a man;
> So be it when I shall grow old.
> Or let me die!

Now the secret of this wonder is suggested in a recently found saying of Jesus: 'Let not him who seeks cease until he finds, and when he finds he shall wonder: wondering, he shall reach the kingdom, and having reached the kingdom he shall rest.' *When he finds he shall wonder.*

This experience of wonder, of awe and veneration, usually leads to two other feelings that superficially contradict or oppose each other. In actual fact they are complementary elements within the experience of awesomeness. The first is a sense of indescribable well-being and peace; of joy and benevolence – a feeling of ecstasy. It can be neither engineered nor wholly communicated to others. It affords glimpses into areas of life normally closed to the insensitive, to those individuals who are so down-to-earth that their minds are earth-bound on principle. To be apprehended by such an experience is to be filled with gratitude and to feel indebted to life. Professing atheists have confessed their frustration on such occasions at being possessed by the very spirit of thankfulness and yet having no one to thank. They have regretted their disbelief in God and then by their very attitude proceeded, so I believe, to commune with him by some other name. However, this is debatable and not the immediate point of issue. All I want to establish now is that the experience of awe sometimes leads to a feeling of indescribable well-being, akin surely to what Christians mean when they talk about the joys of reconciliation to God and peace of mind. But only sometimes. The experience of awe also significantly leads to penitence, even shame. Recall for a moment that father peering into the cot of his new-born child. He is ecstatic, particularly if this is his first-born. Incredulous, he says little, if anything. Feeling happy and proud, he also begins to feel – *unworthy*; ashamed, penitent, and longs to be a better man. Now why? Indeed, how is it possible for two selves to cohabit in the one personality, the one feeling ashamed of the other? Which self is the real man, or is he a bit of both? And against what moral background does he see himself for this feeling of penitence and shame to be induced, a feeling that usually resolves itself in his determination to be worthy of his new responsibility? More particularly, is there any basic difference in *experience* between his sense of shame and the Christian spirit of penitence? They both result in a change of mind; the father determines to be worthy of his child, and the Christian dedicates himself to please God.

In each case the essential requirement was capacity for awe, for awareness of what I can only call the Absolute or the Ultimate. But never mind about names or terms. What matters pre-eminently is that this capacity should be recognized for what it is – evidence of man's encounter with the Reality we evangelicals call God. And it is best developed not by being sought directly, but – as with happiness and peace of mind – by the seeker paying attention to the values that foster it. They are integrity, sincerity, love, justice, compassion, truth; those spiritual qualities which, as we have previously noticed, are most sharply focused in the total life of Jesus. But wherever they are sought, whether by his conscious help or not, they increase awesomeness in the presence of God who doesn't change by being differently named.

# 7

# *God is Community*

I want now to consider the second great attribute that characterized the life of Jesus – his selfless love – in the light first of all
of our involvement with some of the push-outs of our secular
and permissive society. Some of them talked a lot about freedom
and love as a cover for their promiscuous exploitations. They were
amoral, interpreting freedom as permission to indulge their animal
appetites at will. In the main they were pathetic individuals whose
promiscuity was primarily a symptom of their loveless lives. Never
having experienced a truly loving relationship, they did not know
how to love, a different matter from how to make love. Many of
them were maladjusted with serious mental and emotional dis-
orders. Typical was a nineteen-year-old girl whose parents divorced
when she was twelve. She felt that she belonged nowhere. Her
father was brutal, her mother timid. She was on drugs. A lad of
the same age had never known his father and at an early age was
sent to a home for maladjusted children. He felt what he was –
unwanted by almost everybody. Scores of such youngsters were
vagrants, living on the streets in the heart of London. They dossed
in all sorts of places – disused buildings, the undercroft at St
Martin-in-the-Fields, a favourite haunt for daytime sleeping,
Covent Garden, parks, nooks and crannies around Piccadilly – and
dozed at every opportunity in certain all-night coffee bars and
clubs. They resented the police and viewed them as enemies. The
only life they knew was the one they created for themselves within
their own little communities. They lived by conning (the art of
scrounging). Their victims – who offered surprisingly little resist-
ance – were members of the general public. It seemed comparatively easy to beg enough for each day, especially when sharing
among themselves was regulated only by need. If three of them

possessed one cigarette, meaning that one of them had one cigarette and the other two none, they each smoked a third. They shared everything to their last piece of bread and smallest coin. The fundamental reason for this unconditional generosity was their sense of belonging to an accepting community. They *felt* – a most significant word – that they belonged, and this introduced them to feelings that most of us take for granted – security, personal significance, the comfort that we matter to somebody.

Our own early involvement caused us to recognize two important things; the essential meaning of community and the poverty of so much that passed for Christian fellowship. I remember talking to a temporary member of our staff who had emerged from the underworld of alcoholism, drugs, vagrancy, and drifting. She was in her late twenties, the victim of a wretched background. After months of attending our meetings, she was talking to me about a certain aspect of the work we were trying to do. 'You know,' she said, 'I am more conscious of God in the undercroft at St Martin's than I am at Regent Hall.' This was not a criticism of Regent Hall. She loved the place and many of the people who attended; some of them were her friends with whom she worshipped and in whose homes she enjoyed hospitality. What she meant was that in the undercroft she felt more the member of a *Christian* community. The reason was simple. In that community the members accepted each other unconditionally. No questions were asked or demands made. A non-judgmental approach was taken for granted. There were no shocked reactions or anything else faintly resembling censoriousness. Relationships were outgoing and based upon mutual helpfulness. Individuals were accepted on their face value and encouraged to live for today, the operative word being *live*. Within such a community of mutual acceptance the members experienced for the first time something of being loved for themselves alone. Most of them had previously known little but rejection and disapproval. They had not been wanted, a fact made painfully clear to them from their earliest memory. Life had been full of misery and failure, not necessarily because they had come from broken or materially impoverished homes, but because more had been demanded of them than they had been able to give; always more, in terms of behaviour, schooling, home, their place in society. Parents had criticized them and generally made relationships impossible; teachers had pushed them too far or given them up as hopeless; they had failed the eleven-plus, failed to please anyone, been chased by the law, lived at the centre of bickering and family dissension for too long, lost one job after another, and finally concluded that everybody was against them. Some had run away from home and disappeared without trace. They had journeyed to London from most parts of Britain intent upon cutting themselves off from the past and start-ing afresh. Inevitably they had brought their troubles with them. But they had found an accepting community and within it the beginnings of happiness. I have no desire to exaggerate and am fearful that this incomplete picture might give a false impression, but the importance of the community idea cannot be over-stated.

My concern is that we evangelicals have failed to create the sort of communities in which people of all types feel at home. Within our fellowships individuals such as those I have described would feel awkward, intruders, unwanted, rejected; indeed, for such intuitive reasons they stay away. They find more authentic community among themselves, and tend to look upon all outsiders as members of the opposition.

We early realized the importance of fostering this sense of com-munity, of encouraging its spontaneous development, but this obviously demanded that we become insiders, no easy matter. Significantly, the initiative to this end was taken by our young workers themselves, with no prompting from me. They started to wander the streets of Soho and district at all hours of the day and night, notably the latter. For weeks and months they visited clubs, coffee bars, and places already mentioned, their only intention being to get known and if possible accepted. They met many young drifters and were introduced to their small communities, but inevitably the progress was slow and uncertain. Then one of them had a startling idea. Before sharing it with you let me tell you something of his background. He came to London to train in hotel management. Until then he had been a student and a teacher in Scotland, but this proved to be not entirely to his liking, and soon his wanderlust again asserted itself. His new work was fascinating and fast moving, but the city itself was lonely, depres-singly impersonal. One night, sight-seeing or perhaps simply killing time, he walked through Piccadilly and Soho, slowly making his way back to the famous hotel where he was training. It was Tuesday night in the region of nine o'clock. The streets were crowded and noisy. But above the din he heard strains of music played by a brass band. He traced it to a back street in Soho where some thirty Salvationists were taking part in an open-air meeting. The young Scot felt excited and, with time on his hands, gratefully stood to listen. Within five minutes or so, the band secretary, a man well turned seventy years of age and a notorious convert of some fifty years ago, approached him and they began to chat. Their conversation continued for perhaps twenty minutes and shortly before it concluded the band secretary invited the young Scot to a Sunday meeting at Regent Hall. He promised to attend, and did so on the following Sunday morning. The meeting impressed him with its reverent gaiety. Every member of the large congregation appeared to be deeply involved; their singing pulsated with vitality, their prayers were about things near to the young man's need, their testimonies, sometimes haltingly expressed, spoke of a living faith, and even their sometimes rhythmic hand-clapping, which surprised him most of all, seemed naturally to harmonize with the whole happy proceedings. He returned at night and repeatedly over the following weeks. Finally, in a way that surprised no one more than himself, he committed himself to Christ and began to share our programme of community care. Within four months he was knocking on the door of my office asking to be accepted as a member of our full-time voluntary service team. I agreed, but not immediately, wanting to be sure that he realized the seriousness of discontinuing his managerial training.

About eight months after joining us he came up with his startling idea, one born of his deepening involvement with young drifters, drug abusers, and other push-outs. He wanted to start an all-night club. More correctly, he started it. I was on annual holiday at the time and returned to find the venture well under way. He explained that he knew I wouldn't mind! His aim was to gather together under one roof all the young people he now knew through his association on the streets. He believed that the community to which they already loosely belonged needed to develop a ready identity of its own and would do so if allowed simply to evolve at its own speed. The community, it should be explained, already existed in fragmentation; the primary need now was to provide an opportunity for integration and development. In next to no time the all-night club was a swinging success, a fact attributable in no small way to the support of the entire congregation at Regent Hall. Obviously, they could not participate personally, having their own commitments at other points of our extensive programme, but the spirit in which they accepted the real inconvenience of the club's mere existence was in itself an inspiration. For the club made really impossible demands on our limited premises with the result that often its presence was underlined in most unpleasant ways. Sunday-school children found syringes all over the place; canteen facilities used also by Sunday worshippers and other individuals throughout the week were soiled by vomit, urine and other evidence of indiscipline or indifference. It's true that the offenders were not typical, but this hardly helped to make the unpleasantness more bearable. Walls were defaced and items of furniture broken. Despite every effort to keep the premises clean and wholesome for other activities, the members of our staff, all of them young people, sometimes felt that they were fighting a losing battle. But they never despaired, probably because our congregation, far from criticizing them or complaining about the unfortunate results of their work, rallied to their support in countless ways.

The club grew in strength and slowly acquired an identity of its own. It was called the Rink because Regent Hall was a roller-skating rink until converted by the Salvation Army in 1882, and the name stuck through the years. Talk to any Salvationist the world over about the Rink and he will know immediately that you are referring to Regent Hall, the famous Salvation Army centre in the West End of London. This latest addition to its activities – the all-night club – had a simple programme based on the conviction that a formal programme or anything like it was out of the question. The one aim was to create and develop relationships of mutual respect, trust and acceptance. We wanted the young people to feel part of something big and significant that belonged to themselves, a community with which they were proud to be associated, and in which they found, consciously or otherwise, stability and a growing sense of personal value. To this end the night was spent in talking, listening to the record player, eating cheap hot

meals or easy snacks, and generally sharing a common existence.
We quickly learned the futility of trying to talk about religion
formally or informally. Initially we tried, with disastrous results.
Our motives were honourable enough, but the young people
interpreted our efforts as confirmation that we were exploiting
our hospitality for evangelical purposes. This was notably true
when sometimes, at our invitation, we were visited by evangelical pop groups. The young zealots came and interspersed their
playing with words of testimony or short expositions of the
Bible. They insisted that such witness was essential to the central
purpose of their being with us. In the early days we were
inclined to agree, but experience compelled us to think again. The
club members were offended or amused. They left. We found that
customary evangelical methods and anything remotely associated
with them were a barrier and undermined the one aim that concerned us most – the building of an accepting community. Such
an approach was too suggestive of *us* and *them*, of *we* Christians
talking to *you* sinners; and of that spirit of devout Pharisaism
which, as we have already noticed, tends to judge and condemn
people with different (and therefore always lower) moral standards.
Now, to condemn is to reject, and to be rejected is to want to
retaliate, to hit back in the name of rejecting the rejectors. For
these reasons – some of them learned by bitter experience – we
perceived the need to discover another way to communicate our
Christian faith.

Over the years leadership of the club inevitably changed, and
this again introduced new ideas and insights. Incidentally, I should
mention that leadership also changed because I decided that a
maximum of two years was long enough for any young person,
no matter how dedicated, to spend in such an environment. The
Scot left us to attend the national college for youth leadership
training and was succeeded as leader by a twenty-two-year-old
Cambridge graduate. He left us at the end of two years to do
post-graduate studies at a northern university, and we now have
another twenty-two-year-old leader who is assisted by a Salvationist bachelor of science, a Salvationist graduate in sociology,
an ex-trainee teacher who calls herself an agnostic, and a Methodist
who was released by the civil service for twelve months to enable
him to join us. The leader was never new to the work, having

been with us for probably twelve months before being appointed.

Two major developments in the club are worthy of note in the context of this book. Still obsessed with the one aim of building a distinctive community, we were finally driven to the reluctant conclusion that *unconditional* acceptance did not work; it bristled with practical problems beyond our ability to cope. For instance, we discovered that our open door to all-comers admitted the occasional drug-pusher and other equally unscrupulous individuals. They were a disruptive influence in numerous ways, not least in their ability to disintegrate the club and give it an unfortunate reputation. More to the point, their presence was a danger to young people not on drugs. We decided ruthlessly to discriminate. In future, admittance was by membership only, and this was controlled by possession of a card or more usually by the face being known to the doorman who remained at his post throughout most of the night. New members were allowed if introduced by existing members or our own youth leaders. This reduced the size of the community, but immediately paid off in terms of a better club spirit. Increasingly the Rink became a popular rendezvous for members and their friends not only on club nights, but throughout the week. They dropped in to see our workers, sometimes by appointment, or to collect an item or two from our clothing store. They were demanding, but beneath the surface appreciative and co-operative. Their pet hate was any attempt to organize or change them. They wanted freedom, meaning the opportunity to do pretty well as they liked. Throughout the week our workers met them in three distinctive ways; at the all-night club every Friday; during twice-weekly patrols in the early hours of Thursday and Sunday (both patrols consisted of unhurried visitation to popular haunts and started at about ten o'clock on the previous night); and in the undercroft at St Martin's. The latter activity represented real co-operation between this famous Anglican church in Trafalgar Square and the Salvation Army. The vicar, the Rev. Austen Williams, invited us to help by providing workers to assist in the running of the undercroft, part of the crypt set aside to minister to young drifters from nine in the morning until five in the evening, Monday to Saturday. On Sundays it was used as a feeding depot for older vagrants. The daily routine never varied. As soon as the door opened the youngsters moved in.

They slept, listened to non-stop radio one, a background they found indispensable, talked, rested, shared, ate, came and went erratically, and generally prepared for another probably wakeful night. Some of them injected their drugs there as an alternative to using a public lavatory or some such place. One afternoon a week, a Salvation Army doctor held his surgery in the undercroft; his patients needed a variety of treatment both physical and psychological.

However, my purpose is not to analyse this particular aspect of our total involvement. The task is beyond me any way, for my knowledge of it is largely second-hand and therefore superficial in terms of essential detail. The real day-to-day work was done, let me make it clear, by our youth leaders and voluntary helpers. My main contribution was to preside over a weekly staff meeting, during which we thrashed out questions of policy and sometimes discussed case histories, and to consult with my young colleagues at odd times of day and night about their activities generally. I refer to the undercroft primarily to illustrate how and why we became so convinced that the secret of any success we might achieve was centred in the idea of *community*, the fostering of creative relationships within an accepting group. Until this was achieved, little else was possible. The undercroft at St Martin's made a vital contribution to this end; and – perhaps equally important – our united efforts there demonstrated without fuss the ecumenical church in action. We knew little about the thirty-nine articles, and our Anglican friends knew probably less about our articles of war, but such matters proved to be unimportant. We were partners, brothers in a common cause. By working together we discovered that the things that united us were infinitely stronger than the things that in theory should have kept us apart. We worshipped and prayed together without reservation or touchiness as a natural outcome of our co-operation in service. Facing the practicalities of our common commitment, we found that arguments about church order, reformed or renewed liturgies, apostolic succession and much else that likewise occupies countless ecumenical agendas were superseded. We *were* united, members of a Christian family whose total resources, we knew, were behind us all. We didn't argue about theology; we were too busy trying to live it together. Without wishing to minimize the importance of consultations and the like – I've attended more than my share – I have come to believe that the quickest and perhaps the only road to Christian union is via the workshop of mission, not the conference table. However, all this is by the way. I must return to the two major developments in the all-night club.

The first one – our conclusion that unconditional acceptance did not work in our particular situation – we have already considered. The second development was not so much a deliberate decision on our part as a recognition of how the work was evolving spontaneously. We saw the need for what we grandly, but accurately, called therapeutic groups. Within the wider community certain individuals began to emerge with, broadly speaking, one thing in common – the desire to chuck the old life and find something better. Put like that, the impression might be given that they were in some way responding to our message and making a positive decision to be different. This was not the case. They emerged only in the sense that we recognized their need and often unspoken wish for something more than their existing way of life provided. In various ways they intimated that they were ready and desirous of taking a few more steps along the road of rehabilitation; but there was nothing cut and dried about their attitude. It belonged to a twilight world of which they themselves were barely aware. We invited them individually to meet us in groups of three and four, never more than six, for what can probably best be described as recreational evenings. After a simple meal, providing for most of them a rare opportunity to sit round a table and use knives and forks, they engaged in painting and other forms of group activity. Little was planned and nothing was imposed. The young drifters continued to attend as and when they wished; no attempt was made to persuade them back if they withdrew.

Our hope, of course, was that we should learn together more about ourselves and the meaning of mature personal relationships. For this was what life was all about and the area in which, we believed, God was ceaselessly at work. I have repeatedly made it clear that the young push-outs had no interest in institutional religion or Christianity as such. But like all of us they wanted to enjoy life, to live it up, another way of saying that they wanted, again like all of us, to understand the essential nature of self-fulfilment and mutually satisfying relationships. Their interest was practical, not academic. Here, for instance, was Bill whose girl-friend was Jane. They were both inadequate and, as far as they understood, unloved by anyone but each other. They felt insecure, sometimes frightened. Emotionally they leaned on each other to stay upright, but still they fought and wept and occasionally hated each other. To discuss with them the meaning of love was difficult enough; to tell them that God loved them was a sick joke. The only way they could understand love was by being loved. God's love was worse than meaningless to them until they experienced it in and from somebody else. To make preaching a substitute for loving or even to give it first priority was a denial of the gospel, a blasphemy that was not redeemed by its devout intentions.

Needless to say, such an approach was challenging enough for us. We early learned that to talk about God's love in abstract or impersonal terms was little more than a jolly exercise in theological debate or biblical exposition; but to love a maladjusted and sometimes anti-social youngster who hadn't washed for days and who threw your love back in your face was another world, the real one. I get heartily sick of evangelical do-gooders who hand out tracts but never give themselves to people 'not nice to know' on a personal level. They trade in 'stones' while the victims of their misguided zeal continue to ask for 'bread'. Love as revealed by Jesus is something of which most of us know little in theory and less in practice. Perhaps the explanation is that, like all creative gifts, love grows only by being exercised; or – more probable still – we lack the insight and desire of Florence Allshorn when she wrote:

Perhaps God will teach me to love, if I ask hard enough. I feel as if I am not awake yet. I feel as though there is such lots more in me that somehow hasn't got a releasing touch yet ... I used to think that being nice to people and feeling nice was loving people. But it isn't. Love is the most immense unselfishness and it is so big I've never touched it.[1]

We, too, wanted to learn better how to love and were convinced that God would best be able to teach us alongside the members of our all-night club, in the smaller therapeutic groups, and involved in similar situations of sustained personal encounter;

[1] J. H. Oldham, *Florence Allshorn and the Story of St Julian's*, SCM Press 1951, p. 21.

some of us were committed to less colourful aspects of our work, but the general principle held good – we learned to love by loving real persons, warts and all. This was true for us but, from one standpoint at least, more so for the young drifters. For we had the massive influence of our Christian faith and the fellowship of likeminded people to help us; the youngsters had nothing but their instinctive hunger for maturity, another name for capacity to love. And there was one other crucial difference, one which we evangelicals prefer either to overlook or not to see at all. We had a personal relationship with Jesus Christ, a relationship that represented for some of us our most precious possession, the source of everything indispensable to our very existence. Not so the young people, including – for reasons I have already explained – some of our staff members. They found most Jesus-talk either offensive, puzzling, or somewhere between the two. When we talked about personal commitment to Jesus Christ they understood our words but not our meaning. The whole concept of individual salvation was foreign to their community-orientated thinking. It represented a serious contradiction in terms, an attitude both selfish and anti-social. What right had we, they argued, in a world like ours to bother about ourselves, our individual salvation? We should be worrying about Biafra, Vietnam, South Africa, civil rights, racialism and all the other areas of inhumanity. To say that they found our evangelical emphasis upon personal salvation an affront is the proverbial understatement of the century. They quoted it to illustrate their insistence that the church was a corrupting influence; that its preoccupation with its own structures merely reflected the attitude of its average member to life in general. Of course such comments were too extreme, but they contained too many germs of truth to be ignored.

My thinking on this whole vital matter was helped considerably, first of all, by Harvey Cox in *On not leaving it to the Snake*. He wrote:

Protestant piety had reduced the dimensions of the Christian claim. We have taken the earliest Christian affirmation 'Jesus Christ is Lord', a confession which expresses the exultant sweep and cosmic scope of God's intention, and substituted for it the pietistic diminutive, 'I accept Jesus as personal Saviour'. Though the latter phrase is insisted on most tenaciously by those who claim to be closest to the Bible, the phrase itself never appears in the New Testament and there is little scriptural justification for it. It reduces the cosmic claims of the gospel to the manageable dimensions of an inward individualism.[1]

This was evocative enough, but then I came across the following comment by Bishop F. R. Barry in his book, *Secular and Supernatural*. Having quoted the above passage, he observed:

What is called 'deciding for Christ' at revival meetings has, I should say, little immediate relevance to the real situation of Christians in such a society as we know today. What is meant by 'christianizing' that society is not only, and perhaps not primarily, a concern for individual 'conversions'. It is more, much more, humble and patient labour, in co-operation with our fellow-citizens who may not call themselves by the name 'Christian', in working out a viable social ethic and attempting to bring the structures of society into closer accord with Christian principles, to serve and to safeguard freedom, justice and brotherhood.

He concluded:

The denunciation of teenage promiscuity does nothing to set forward the reign of Christ. It is rather a matter of getting Christian insights more effectively embodied in the social order, helping people to find their way towards them and showing that Christian principles of living are in fact the ways in which life does work best, the ways to being most truly human.[2]

How remarkable that the retired bishop's quiet reflections, based of course upon a lifetime of pastoral over-sight and real caring, and our noisy involvement with young drifters in the West End of London should lead to the same conviction, one which for us particularly carried revolutionary implications. There is no doubt in my mind that for many years to come numerous individuals will find Christ as I did, and within that experience discover personal direction and fulfilment; but I am equally sure that far more people will experience the same Reality in community – sharing common activities and learning together what it means to live and to love, thereby exploring what the bishop calls 'ways to being most truly human'. Certainly this was how we proceeded with the young push-outs; there was no other way.

[1] SCM Press 1968, pp. 97f.    [2] SCM Press 1969, pp. 62f.

And, increasingly, our involvement with entirely different types of people intimated that the same community or group emphasis was essential. In a number of significant ways it largely superseded the individualistic approach that until now had dominated our evangelism and social service.

The flower children's club was a case in point. It met every Sunday night from eight o'clock until about eleven, bringing together young people from many parts of suburban London. They created their own community, one to which they were grateful and I think proud to belong. There was no formal programme. The members engaged in such activities as discussion, music making, poetry reading, debates, dialogues, and – most popular of all – nothing in particular. They simply liked being together, feeling part of something bigger than themselves or even the sum total of their individual contributions. The group gave them emotional stability and a sense of direction or aim. It included a minority of 'professional hippies', youngsters who conned a living and gave all their time to the cause of flower-power, but most of the members were basically indistinguishable from the less flamboyant young people with whom they associated at school and work. They were united by the idealism of their cult, which in a number of ways represented religionless Christianity. At least the theory did; the practice was sometimes a different matter. But the sincerity of the young people was convincing and inspiring. They wanted to change the world. Their protest was a rejection of materialism with its phony values and priorities, and a plea that society should learn to live like a loving family. This was in some ways rather surprising, for not a few of them were unhappy at home and appeared to be most misunderstood there. Their parents were suspicious of their ideas and disapproving of their dress. Some of the parents appeared never to have the time – or perhaps the inclination – to sit down to *listen*. The situation in many homes was one of silent belligerence or unhearing condemnation. The young people often wanted to talk to their parents, to explain their ideas and to seek advice, but the opportunity was almost never given.

After eighteen months we decided to close the club for a reason which at its inception and for months immediately afterwards would have been inconceivable. The flower children were now

too orthodox to warrant or even to support a distinctive club of
their own. They had outgrown the need for many of the symbols
of flower-power idealism, but not the idealism itself. They were
just as committed, in less unorthodox ways, to 'make love, not
war', a popular slogan of the time. Now without wishing to give
the impression that their ideas about love with which they usually
associated sex were identical with ours, many of them sought to
understand loving relationships beyond the context of sexuality
alone. This was one subject in which there was general interest;
a ready talking-point for all occasions. During such discussions we
discovered fundamental misunderstandings of Christian teaching.
Some of the young people thought of discipline, for example, as
the enemy of freedom, and of liberty as licence. They also interpreted self-denial as self-hatred, the attitude that encourages self-
destruction through self-condemnation, self-despising and the like.
We sought to explore the mind of Christ on such matters and to
show how different was his approach to those very areas of human
experience in which the majority of our youthful secularists were
most interested. These discussions were anything but a crafty
imposition on our part. They were spontaneous developments of
deepening relationships, a fact I cannot emphasize too strongly.
And we never felt that we were propagating Christianity as such.
We were, like our young friends, simply talking about life, so-
called secular life, which explains my conviction, not theirs, that
Christ was intimately involved. For if, as we Christians have
always claimed, he was the unique revelation of love, then his
teaching, understood as such or not, was relevant to people
seeking insight into the nature and fulfilment of love at the points
of life that mattered most to them – friendships, home, job,
leisure. So we talked about the meaning of his life and teaching in
largely secular terms. We saw, for instance, that one of love's
basic principles was defined by Jesus when he said that we must
lose life to find it; die to live. Again, indirectly through his eyes,
we saw that to love others we must first love ourselves. 'Love your
neighbour,' he said, 'as you love yourself.' Yet how many people
imagine that self-love is the opposite of love for others? They
mistake love for self as inevitably selfish and self-centred, not
realizing that true love for self is expressed in self-respect and
self-acceptance. Some of us even indulge in self-hate crusades

to prove the extent of our love for God or people, or both. The four gospels, on the other hand, explicitly and implicitly indicate that some of us cannot love others because we do not love ourselves enough and in the right way. We show little respect because we have no self-respect; are estranged from others through self-alienation; criticize innocent victims to relieve our own self-condemnation. These are the things about which Jesus talked; and they are the self-same realities that exercise the minds of countless individuals today, though in thought-forms apparently far removed from considerations of God and the things that belong to his kingdom. This being so, all sorts of people think about God by some other name far more than they realize. And is it not true that their very seeking after truth, whatever its spiritual or moral nature, indicates that they are already in touch with the truth they seek?

I believe that Jesus helps us uniquely to understand selfless love; he exemplifies it in his life and clarifies its essential nature in his teaching. This quality of love, like the spiritual dimension to which we have already referred, points to a source beyond itself. Jesus's whole life, apart from his words, said so repeatedly; and he called that source God. But the name is important only as a means of ready identification. What really matters is the source itself and our understanding of it. Paul Tillich sometimes called it depth, and this caused him to write in his book *The Shaking of the Foundations*:

That depth is what the word God means. And if that word has not much meaning for you, translate it, and speak of the depths of your life, of the source of your being, of your ultimate concern, of what you take seriously without any reservation. Perhaps, in order to do so, you must forget everything traditional that you have learned about God, perhaps even the word itself. For if you know that God means depth, you know much about him. You cannot then call yourself an atheist or unbeliever. For you cannot think or say: Life has no depth! Life itself is shallow! He who knows depth knows about God.[1]

I recognize, of course, that to say God is love is rather different from saying love is God, but this does not alter the fact that to experience a truly loving relationship is to be in touch with God,

[1] SCM Press 1949; Pelican Books, pp. 63f.

the source of all love. Explanations and terms are secondary by comparison with such living knowledge. Yet we evangelicals often insist upon *starting* with the love of God; talking about it, I mean, as though, if the conventional terminology associated with it is not immediately used, we are being untrue to the gospel itself. When we can't get a hearing, we blame our hoped-for converts for not listening! But many of them will listen and share lively discussion when the subject is not God, at least by that name initially, but love. Perhaps, on the other hand, they don't want to *talk* about God or love at all. Their interest is in *living*; in real people and real justice for real people. Their business is experience, not exposition. And their very sincerity means that they and professing Christians have much in common, certainly too much to justify endless squabbles over whether God is known only when identified in strictly religious terms.

# 8

## *God is Responsibility*

We come now to the third great attribute of Jesus – his sense of ultimate accountability. This was the background against which he lived and died; the touchstone of judgment to which he brought every decision. It gave his life direction and urgency. 'I must work while it is day,' he said, 'the night comes when no man can work.' But this drive was not the reaction of fear, a frantic effort to win God's favour and deserve his love. It was the eager obedience of faith in the ultimate invincibility of God's purpose. 'For Christ suffered for you,' wrote the author of 'First Peter', 'and left you a personal example, and wants you to follow in his steps.... When he was insulted he offered no insult in return. When he suffered he made no threats of revenge. *He simply committed his cause to the One who judges fairly*.'[1] Jesus neither expected nor demanded immediate personal vindication or the fruits of public success. Believing that ultimate victory was certain, he interpreted temporal affairs in the light of eternal realities. For he was a citizen of two worlds, and loyal to both at one and the same time.

Unfortunately some of his most zealous followers have at times interpreted his teaching about 'last things' largely in terms of fear. They have talked of God's judgment in threatening tones, seeking to intimidate their listeners to 'flee from the wrath to come'. God has been depicted as a vindictive bully who shows more interest in punishment than penitence. The result is that modern secular man finds it virtually impossible to take seriously the church's traditional emphasis upon life beyond the grave. The emphasis is right, and Christianity is incomplete without it, but irrevocable harm has been done by false teachers. They have talked of heaven and hell with the supposed omniscience of God

[1] I Peter 2.21-23 (J. B. Phillips' version).

himself, and reduced the whole vital matter to one of ridicule deserving only of contempt.

When initially we associated with some of the young people I have described, they referred to what they imagined to be the church's teaching about God's judgment as another rather sick joke; and as ample evidence that the Christian religion itself was phony. You can't expect intelligent people, they said, to bother about all that hell-fire stuff. It was this underlying assumption that Christianity was outdated, a relic of man's twilight exploration for truth, that defeated our efforts to talk about our faith. Put like that, it probably looks as though we were on the prowl again to impose our religion upon every unsuspecting person prepared to listen; that we were obsessed with the idea of 'bearing witness' to justify our involvement with the young people. But it wasn't like that at all, as I have previously explained. Our concern was to encourage real encounter, face to face, mind to mind, heart to heart, but so often we found that erroneous ideas about the faith we represented ruled this out or at least made it more difficult. Many of these ideas, representing half-truth or no truth at all, were centred on distortions of the church's teaching about heaven and hell. And what distortions! God alone knows their origins; it is surely inconceivable that Sunday-school or the class-room is wholly to blame. But until they are countered – and personal dialogue seems the only way – we evangelicals face insurmountable barriers. However, the point I want to underline is that for such reasons Christianity itself was thought to be antiquated, unreal, nonsensical, unrelated to life. It didn't deserve serious discussion, being too other-worldly to be true anyway. The situation appeared stalemate.

We began to find our way through the impasse with the help once more of Harvey Cox. He will never know how much his book *The Secular City* helped us, from a practical standpoint. I am not competent to argue about its final theological merit, but I can testify that some of its ideas worked in helping us to talk about what was real and meaningful to young people normally indifferent to conventional Christianity.

We speak of God politically [wrote Harvey Cox] whenever we give occasion to our neighbour to become the responsible, adult agent, the fully post-town and post-tribal man God expects him to be today. We speak to him of God whenever we cause him to realize consciously the web of interhuman reciprocity in which he is brought into being and sustained in it as a man. We speak to him of God whenever our words cause him to shed some of the blindness and prejudices of immaturity and to accept a larger and freer role in fashioning the instrumentalities of human justice and cultural vision. We do not speak to him of God by trying to make him religious but, on the contrary, by encouraging him to come fully of age, putting away childish things.[1]

It all seems so obvious now, but at the time that comment opened up for us new vistas of truth and in consequence a new vocabulary for talking about God. Until then, we had started, as it were, at the Godward end. Our approach had been: 'God loves you; be reconciled to him.' Not surprisingly we made no headway; most of our conversations were stillborn or killed at birth. But now, prompted by Harvey Cox's insight, our emphasis was upon responsible living, upon giving our neighbour occasion to become a 'responsible, adult agent'. For almost without exception the young people, we learned, wanted to be responsible. Indeed, this was their motivation in supporting moral causes and fighting for their concept of social justice. Their critics, the people who find long hair and unconventional clothes an affront, will, I realize, dismiss the whole idea as ridiculous and perhaps as even irresponsible. They will point to the drop-outs and drug abusers and hippies and other individuals they sometimes call 'social parasites' as examples of how not to live responsibly; and, in so doing, they will illustrate not only their own misunderstanding based upon second-hand information, but the folly, if Harvey Cox is right, of such an attitude expressing its disapproval in orthodox religious terms. For to talk in such a way is to make it more difficult, not less, for people to become responsible, adult agents.

Incidentally, a moment's reflection will confirm the possibility of Christian concern degenerating into devout do-goodism, and nothing makes responsible living more difficult for the victims than that. Yet in our understandable desire to be useful, we evangelicals are inclined to do things for people instead of helping them to do things for themselves. We are suckers for a con if only because helping people is our business, the natural result of our acceptance of Christian obligation. But to be kind in terms

[1] Harvey Cox, *The Secular City*, SCM Press 1965; Pelican Books, p. 265.

of, for instance, giving money – whether to alcoholic, vagrant or some other inadequate personality – is a poor substitute for real caring; taking time to sit down to listen, to become possibly deeply involved in an attempt to find basic causes for the inadequacy and the means of finding lasting solutions. There is, of course, no doubt that material help is often urgently needed – and rightly takes priority over everything else – but to give *things* as distinct from giving *ourselves* is to encourage irresponsible living and to make it more difficult for the individual concerned to grow up. He receives so much help, help lacking in insight, that his juvenile dependence is strengthened and made attractive. Beyond his knowing, he develops a vested interest in prolonging his dependence and is conditioned to think of himself as inadequate. Sometimes he *is* inadequate, with built-in personality deficiencies for which he is not responsible, but more often his attitude of pathetic helplessness is the easiest answer he knows to the challenge of life.

We met such people, but they were not typical. Most of our young secularists wanted to be responsible, though this was hardly the language they used. Superficially their way of life was a blatant contradiction of their verbose idealism. They appeared to be anti-social, not infrequently making life difficult for the police and other representatives of law and order. They were critical of most things conventional, priding themselves on being non-conformists, something their gregarious existence and slavish submission to changing fashion denied. They were contemptuous of the rat race, perhaps because it revealed for some of them their fear of personal mediocrity. But making allowance for all this and much more that could be said, we were convinced beyond doubt that most of the young people we knew wanted desperately to be responsible. Their very way of life, the one so deplored by many of their elders, was, they argued, an evidence of true responsibility, for it protested against the crude materialism of the society they had inherited and wanted to change. Here was paradox indeed! These youthful rejectors of institutional religion were fighting, they believed, for spiritual values. Obviously, they used other terms, but as we listened to them – to their passionate arguments about an earthly utopia – we heard in modern jargon re-echoes of New Testament evaluations and emphases. They cared about many of the things near to the heart of Jesus Christ. I have no desire to overstate the case. They were not paragons; far from it. A tiny majority of them were unashamedly concerned about themselves alone. Many of them were sadly misguided, despite their undoubted sincerity. But the vast majority of them were responsible or trying to be; and this was our common living and talking point, for we, too, wanted to be responsible.

First, however, we had to perceive the meaning of responsibility in today's world. We older people thought we knew, but the young people disagreed and were not afraid to say so. They insisted that authoritarianism must give way to authenticity; that a thing was not real or valid merely because tradition said so; that the authoritative was self-evident and not the prerogative of people with authority. This led them to defy authoritarianism in the home, at school and college, at work, in the church and the Establishment generally. Parents were distressed, authorities infuriated, and relationships between the old and the young made complex, tense and sometimes explosive. The reason was not the young's disrespect for their elders, though undoubtedly most of them had finally rejected the normally unchallenged idea that wisdom and insight were measured in years, usually called experience. No, the reason behind the young people's defiance of authoritarianism was their concern for society, their passion to remedy wrongs, their protest against exploitation and every form of social injustice. Their refusal to conform, like their awkwardness generally, was – making allowances for possible less commendable secondary causes – their wish to be responsible. We shall never understand the phenomenon of modern youth in revolt, often fierce and violent revolt, until we recognize that they believe themselves to be engaged in a moral crusade, fighting for a changed society and a better world. Their best resources – enthusiasm, zest, initiative – they often use against themselves by over-simplifying the causes of the wrongs they oppose. Almost invariably they underestimate the sinfulness of man, his inveterate self-centredness and failure to match his moral development with his scientific and technological achievements. Many of them have the aptitude for thinking that sincerity of purpose is virtually the same thing as sound or even infallible judgment, and this encourages naïvety and a spirit of intolerance. They tend to consider themselves the freedom fighters and their opponents the reactionaries whose only

concern is self-interest. The measures they adopt to assert themselves are sometimes more the harbingers of anarchy than the
expressions of democracy. And by occasionally using a sledge-
hammer of protest to crack a nut of contention, they create misunderstanding and disproportionate antagonism against themselves.
But basically, I repeat, they are not irresponsible. Their appearances – clothes, hair, attitudes – that cause so much offence to
older people are, we found on closer examination, expressions of
dissatisfaction with society and a longing to change it. Of course
their words often outpace their deeds or replace them altogether,
but this failing is not restricted to young idealists.

Now this word responsibility implies that some sort of response
is involved. But to what or to whom? The question, like the answer,
is important, for the whole of life, its depth and direction, is
measured in terms of response. We are alive only to the extent
that we respond to people and things. They remain meaningless
and insignificant until they evoke a response within us. The
degree of our response is the measure of our involvement. If we
remain insensitive – whether to beauty, pain, sorrow, injustice,
nobility, privilege, obligation – we are that much less alive, less
aware, and incapable of responsible living. Our young friends were
engaged in their moral and social protests as a result of their
response to what Paul Tillich called 'ultimate concern'. They did
not believe in God; their attempts to live responsibly were not
inspired by any conscious response to him or to what they con-
ceived to be his will. But some of their ultimate concerns were in
harmony with the objective revelation of God in the person of
Jesus Christ. This meant that they and we were defining our
understanding of responsible living by referring to the same, or
to very similar, criteria of judgment. Incredible though it may
seem, not until now had we realized that human responsibility
was a major emphasis in the New Testament. This had not been our
usual interpretative approach. We had concentrated rather on
seeking to understand what God had done for us, on reading the
Scriptures both to prove and to cultivate our own devoutness; and
thereby we had failed to perceive that a large element in the
teaching of Jesus was simply a study in responsible living. His
parable about the Good Samaritan, for instance, carried no reference to God; indeed the orthodox Jews to whom the parable was

first told doubtless found it hard to believe that the Samaritan was capable of belief in God at all, certainly of any valid or saving belief. But this outcast of orthodox religious society met with the approval of Jesus because he so whole-heartedly responded to the needs of a fellow human being, irrespective of race and religion. Unlike the priest and the Levite, whose imagined response to God caused them not to respond to the victim of the attack, the Samaritan did respond to the man and thereby, consciously or otherwise, he responded to God. In each case, the nature of the response determined the degree of the commitment, another name for responsibility.

Jesus called men to be responsible; they were to give and share and sacrifice for the sake of others; to heal the sick, feed the hungry, clothe the naked, visit the prisoner, care for the widow and orphan. They were to be responsible in a world of occupying powers, racial discrimination, social injustice, religious bigotry, and other affronts to human dignity.

We have already seen that responsibility implies response; and we were increasingly sure that we and the young secularists were responding to largely the same values. Ours were centred in God, theirs in people; ours were defined by the revelation of Christ, theirs by their experience of human relationships and life itself. The two approaches were not mutually exclusive, obviously so, but they were distinctive and for the young people further evidence that God was superfluous. So he was, by that name. But if their ultimate concerns were, beyond their knowing, intimations of the mind of Christ, are we not justified in assuming that they were inspired by the same Spirit of truth to whom Jesus bore witness? The final answer to this question is, I realize, wholly dependent upon the young people's total view of life as represented by their ultimate concerns. Otherwise the hard-core secularist – the indivi-dual who in fact as well as by profession has truly embraced secularism – has every reason to accuse me of dishonesty and to claim that I am distorting, if not prostituting, the Christian faith by identifying it with nothing more than responsible living. He could rightly argue that every self-respecting individual, Christian or not, is intent upon responsible living; and that Christians have not been conspicuously more successful than non-Christians in achieving it. He might even go on to suggest that Christianity, with its persecutions, heresy hunts, and other exhibitions of pious depravity, has at times fostered most peculiar ideas about what it means to be responsible. I get his point and readily concede it, having no desire to defend the indefensible. But I must insist that the Christian's definition of responsible living is utterly different from the secularist's, a fact we shall see best, I think, from the standpoint of what each believes about the essential nature of man.

All too often we hear man described as an animal, perhaps because so often he behaves like one. But Christianity insists that he is infinitely more than an animal; he is a trinity of body, mind and spirit or soul; he came from God and returns to God; he has within himself a spiritual kingdom the laws of which, if obeyed, permit communion with God and open the door to experiences within a dimension of life which the secularist denies altogether. He thinks of man in physical and material terms, which means that aesthetic experience is restricted to its animal origins. But many young people, despite their rejection of God and institutional religion, continue to think of life in largely spiritual terms. They read books on eastern religions; try to learn the art of transcendental meditation; wear traditional symbols of faith; use drugs in their quest for Reality or self-fulfilment, a significant fact to which we shall return; sing protest songs about spiritual values; and join occult societies.

Today [wrote John Wren-Lewis] a whole generation is beginning to rebel – sometimes against science itself – because it finds materialistic dogmatism becoming a new intellectual tyranny, not only in the obvious forms like marxism, but equally in the kind of 'tough-talking' outlook of many Western intellectuals who insist that feelings of the numinous or of transcending ordinary physical existence must be dismissed as merely wishful because they have no reality in an essentially material universe.

Mr Wren-Lewis also observed:

The truth is that what we are witnessing today is a revival of interest not in religious belief but in religious experience – or more accurately we are witnessing a growing refusal to dismiss certain kinds of experience which seem personally important, such as experiences of 'the numinous' or of 'immortal longings', simply because they appear to conflict with the common materialistic beliefs of modern Western society. The new interest in religious and spiritual matters has, in fact, little or nothing in common with the theological dogmatism which made church people oppose the discoveries of science from Galileo to the 'Monkey Trial' in the United States in 1925; its spirit is much more that of the scientific pioneers who had to struggle against that dogmatism, for they, too, were fighting for the right to take experience seriously in spite of prevalent beliefs.[1]

This being the case, it is apparent that these young people will have ideas about responsibility different from those held by secularists; for, as we have already noticed, our understanding of responsibility is determined by our response to our ultimate concerns. The Christian or theist interprets his responsibility in the world in terms of his response to God; the young people, those without conscious faith in God, in terms of their response to human values which take cognizance of man's total nature including his spirituality; and the secularist in terms of his response to one main criterion – how best to secure maximum happiness for the maximum number of human animals. Obviously the first two categories largely overlap whereas the third category is distinctive; and this makes a profound difference in the search for a definition of responsibility. For if the secularist's absolute touchstone of moral values is maximum happiness for the maximum number then, apart from considerations of what happens to the minority who go to the wall, sacrificed for the happiness of the greater number, human happiness and therefore the means that make it possible assume pre-eminent importance, even at the cost of integrity, truth, fidelity, honour, and other moral and spiritual values that stand in the way. Individuals who have put principle before convenience and preferred death to dishonour have been misguided idealists indeed, pathetic fools deserving of pity as much as admiration. There are, of course, many other areas in which the essential difference between Christian and secularistic evaluations of life is sharply illustrated, and some of them will emerge as the book proceeds, but enough has already been said to justify the assumption that the difference is fundamental and irreconcilable.

Now if the Christian and the individual with no conscious faith in God seek from the same perspective to understand the meaning of responsible living and in consequence experience together the same

[1] 'Looking for your Guru', from *The Guardian* (1969). See also *The New Reformation?* by John A. T. Robinson, SCM Press 1965.

sense of 'ought', of obligation, of commitment to, the same ultimate concerns, it is surely feasible that no matter how different
their vocabularies they are in essence talking about the same things,
serving the same cause, and are dedicated to the same values. In
this sense there is a real connection between Christian awareness
of ultimate accountability and the kind of commitment to ultimate
concerns that characterizes the attitude of so many young people
in Britain today. Their deepening sense of responsibility is, I
believe, their response to God by some other name. They serve
him beyond their knowing and are inspired by the same spiritual
resources that nourish the faith of more orthodox believers.

To such matters we shall turn in the next chapter, but first let
me attempt a brief summing up of the matters we have considered
in this and the two previous chapters. We said that three attributes
of Jesus's life were his capacity for awe, his attitude of selfless
love, and his awareness of ultimate accountability. We went on
to see that these three attributes had their counterparts in the
*experience* of many young people who make no profession of
faith in God and have rejected the very idea of God by that name.
They, too, are capable of profound wonder in the face of life's
mysteries, the sort of astonished joy that is akin to reverence,
veneration, thanksgiving, and penitence. They, too, care desperately about people, revealing often, beneath appearances of
indifference and worse, degrees of compassion and tenderness that
challenge our sometimes unrealized complacency. They too are
committed to ultimate concerns that bespeak the mind of Christ,
a commitment they work out rarely with reference to abstract
argument, but always to actual personal relationships. It is this commitment to people that causes them to do the responsible thing.

Then are we not justified in believing that God is at work in
their lives, using them in ways they do not at the moment perceive, and seeking through them to open new windows of truth,
thereby leading us all to a greater understanding of both himself and
our own spirituality?

# 9

# God's Grace and Secular Society

In his book *The Cost of Discipleship*, Dietrich Bonhoeffer makes it
clear that the grace of God is free, but not cheap. 'Cheap grace,'
he said, 'means grace sold on the market like cheapjack's wares.'
He continued:

> Grace is represented as the church's inexhaustible treasury, from which she
> showers blessings with generous hands, without asking questions or fix-
> ing limits. Grace without price; grace without cost! The essence of grace,
> we suppose, is that the account has been paid in advance; and, because
> it has been paid, everything can be had for nothing. Since the cost was
> infinite, the possibilities of using and spending it are infinite. What would
> grace be if it were not cheap?[1]

Bonhoeffer was pointing to the paradox that God's grace, like
all his gifts, has to be earned or deserved. We sometimes talk, for
instance, about a gifted musician, meaning that he has outstanding capacity for music-making. Listening to him, we are left in no
doubt about his gift, but at the same time we realize something of
the price he has paid to develop it: the long hours of practice, the
self-discipline, the fastidious attention to detail, the tenacity in
weariness, the dedication to perfection. These things flowed from
the gift and were indispensable to its development. Without them
it would have atrophied and become an indictment. Such gifts
are free – as their recipients readily testify – but they are never
cheap.

It will be helpful to bear this in mind as we consider the grace

[1] SCM Press 1948. Revd. ed. (1959), p. 35.

of God in secular society; his initiative in seeking to help fallen man, man the sinner at war with himself. Christianity has always insisted that we cannot work *for* our own salvation; it must be worked *out*. For salvation is basically concerned with a loving relationship between God and man, and this can never be deserved or earned. It is always a free gift, the consummation of God's loving initiative which also alone explains the presence in the believer's life of what the apostle Paul called the 'harvest of the Spirit – love, joy, peace, patience, kindness, goodness, fidelity, gentleness, and self-control' (Gal. 5.22-23, NEB). With this in mind – the idea that such moral fruits must have spiritual roots – a number of devout Christians have concluded that logically the claim that people live the Christian life without conscious faith in God is disproved. They have argued that without deliberately cultivated transcendental relationships people are incapable of living in the spirit of Christ, of growing characters marked by, to quote the Archbishop of Canterbury's words again, 'an awe-inspiring self-forgetfulness, compassion, humility and courage'. The reasoning behind such a point of view is understandable enough. These devout believers, thinking of their own struggles to achieve anything remotely resembling holiness – struggles inspired by their faith in God and reinforced by all the means of grace made available by the church, not to mention the most vital factor of all, their personal knowledge of Christ – have reached the conviction that without such aids spiritual progress so hardly won is surely impossible. To suggest otherwise is to undermine the whole concept of original sin and to believe that man has outgrown his need for God. All this talk, they further argue, about young people, despite their indifference to God and institutional religion, exemplifying Christian virtues like love and compassion is dangerous nonsense and calculated to make the situation more confused.

Perhaps we shall best get to the heart of the matter by turning immediately to the New Testament. You probably remember the incident, recorded in John 5.1-15, of Jesus healing the man at the Sheep-Pool in Jerusalem. A cripple for thirty-eight years, he waited at the pool for the waters to be disturbed, believing that if on such an occasion he could get in first he would be cured. Jesus surprisingly asked him if he wanted to be healed. Perhaps not without indignation, the man explained that, unable to help himself, he had no one to put him into the pool, whereupon Jesus said: 'Rise to your feet, take up your bed and walk.' We are told that the cripple recovered instantly, turning the symbol of his previous impotence into a sign of his new strength; he carried his bed or stretcher as he began to walk. The accredited religious leaders were furious, for by carrying his bed the healed man was guilty of breaking the Sabbath law. They asked for an explanation of his apparent profanity, and he told them that he was simply obeying the man who had healed him. 'Who is the man?' they asked. Who indeed? For 'the cripple who had been cured *did not know*; the place was crowded and Jesus had slipped away'.

Now their name is legion who have been healed or helped by Christ beyond their own realization. Think for a moment of our London hospitals whose names indicate their Christian foundations: St Thomas's, St Mary's, St Bartholomew's, St George's and so on. Their healing ministries originated in Christian conviction and even today are largely sustained by the same dynamic. Over the centuries countless individuals within their walls have been healed in the name of Christ without their thinking of him at all. He has touched them through the dedicated skill of surgeon and nurse. The same argument applies to other institutions of humanitarianism. How many men, women and children stay, for instance, within the care of the Salvation Army without a moment's thought for the Christ in whose name they are served? How many nameless Christians, unhonoured and largely unnoticed, unconsciously enrich the life of society which nevertheless only at best nods a grateful acknowledgment and ignores completely the real source of its good fortune? The pages of the New Testament, like those of Christian and so-called secular history, are full of illustrations of how Christ helps people beyond their personal awareness in a variety of ways, some of them seemingly secular. He said that 'man cannot live on bread alone; he lives on every word that God utters' (Matt. 4.4, NEB). Significantly, God appears to be far less concerned than are many of his children, notably we evangelicals, about the source of such utterances being always known and suitably acknowledged. Jesus, it is true, is *the* Word made flesh, the unique revelation of God in finite terms; but there are many other 'words' spoken by God, often outside the context of orthodox religion. After all, a word communicates an idea, and ideas are sometimes conveyed most tellingly without any form of verbalization; indeed, words frequently stand in the way of truth. A sunset is not enhanced by a well-meaning commentator trying to describe it. If he is a poet he might manage not to offend, but his best efforts will fall far short of the sunset itself; which explains why such beauty is usually viewed in silence. The soul is nourished, the imagination fired, and what Christians call grace begins to flow. It matters little whether the 'word' is accredited to God, for it still does its cleansing and strengthening work though possibly thought of in non-religious terms.

Such 'words' are often loud and clear as coming from God; music, poetry, drama, books, people, the kind of things Dr William Sangster had in mind when he wrote a suggested prayer for some of his friends:

Slow me down, Lord!
Ease the pounding of my heart by the quieting of my mind.
Steady my hurried pace with a vision of the eternal reach of time.
Give me, amidst the confusion of my day, the calmness of the ever-lasting hills.
Break the tension of my nerves and muscles with the soothing music of the singing streams that live in my memory.
Help me to know the magical restoring power of sleep.
Teach me the art of taking minute vacations ... of slowing down to look at a flower, to chat with a friend, to pat a dog, to read a few lines from a good book.
Remind me each day of the fable of the hare and the tortoise that I may know that the race is not always to the swift; that there is more to life than measuring its speed.
Let me look upward into the branches of the towering oak, and know that it grew great and strong because it grew slowly and well.
Slow me down, Lord, and inspire me to send my roots deep into the soil of life's enduring values that I may grow towards the stars of my enduring destiny.[1]

But there are many less obvious 'words' from God. C. S. Lewis, an atheist at the time, heard one as he idly picked up and read an atheistic journal. Its unconvincing arguments caused him seriously for the first time to doubt his anti-theistic position and set him on a course that led finally to his becoming probably the most

[1] *Dr Sangster* by Paul Sangster, Epworth Press 1962, p. 342.

effective Christian apologist of his day. What a surprising context for an authentic word from God – the pages of a journal intended to affirm that he did not exist! Another such word was surely uttered by Bertrand Russell on his eightieth birthday. Asked what he thought was the greatest asset a man could have in life, this life-long militant agnostic replied:

The root of the matter is a very simple and old-fashioned thing, a thing so simple that I am almost ashamed to mention it, for fear of the derisive smile with which wise cynics will greet my words. The thing I mean – please forgive me for mentioning it – is love, Christian love. If you feel this you have a motive for existence, a guide in action, a reason for courage, an imperative necessity for intellectual honesty ... and although you may not find happiness, you will never know the despair of those whose life is aimless and void of purpose.

To those with ears to hear, the source of such a testimony in no way detracts from the truth of the testimony itself. And why? Because truth is one, which means that whatever its declared label – atheism, humanism, Buddhism, agnosticism, Judaism or any other 'ism' – it harmonizes with God, the source of all truth, and thereby releases in the lives of those it apprehends the dynamic that feeds spiritual freedom. This is not to say, of course, that each of these 'isms' contains the same element of truth or is wholly free of error. Obviously all of them, so Christians believe, fall short of the truth about God as revealed by Christ, but in so far as they reflect the mind or perspective of Christ they minister to that extent to the soul of man. Is it not apparent that individuals like Albert Schweitzer, an unorthodox apostle of Christian self-renunciation; Mahatma Gandhi, a Hindu; Gilbert Murray, a humanist; Herbert Read, an unbelieving seeker after God; Simone Weil, a Christian mystic outside the church; and Martin Buber, a Jewish scholar, all of them revealing rare qualities of personal sanctity, shared a common commitment to truth wherever they found it, and a large degree of insight! This surely means that whether they realized it or not they were keeping company with the One who said, 'If you dwell within the revelation I have brought, you are indeed my disciples; you shall know the truth, and the truth will set you free' (John 8.31-32, NEB). In the area of overlap between different systems of religious, moral, and spiritual teaching, people are consciously and unconsciously dwelling within the revelation that Jesus brought; and thereby, again consciously or otherwise, opening their lives to the grace of God. The source of truth is the same; the channels for its mediation vary considerably.

We evangelicals sometimes give the impression that God's grace is permitted to operate only by our correct response in faith to the spoken gospel; as though God's loving initiative in seeking to make us real persons was controlled by our mental assent to the right sort of theological definitions. For too long we have insisted that God's main – if not only – approach to sinful man has been through the door marked doctrinal belief, meaning of course our inflexible interpretation of biblical revelation. But the ingenuity of infinite love is not so restricted. The grace of God is made available to us in a rich variety of ways, all of them consistent with the biblical revelation, but some of them belonging to what we misguidedly call the secular.

The essential requirement that keeps the channel of God's grace open to us in all situations is the right attitude to life rather than the right set of theological beliefs, though ideally the two are identical. What else was Jesus talking about when he said to the most devout religionists of his day: 'I tell you this: tax-gatherers and prostitutes are entering the kingdom of God ahead of you' (Matt. 21.31, NEB)? The remark sounds insulting and offensive, as undoubtedly it was to its first hearers; but Jesus was obviously trying to shock them into an examination of their bigoted self-righteousness. Their attitude to God, to other people and themselves was wrong, which meant that the direction of both their thinking and living was off course; and direction inevitably determines ultimate destination. The matter was urgent and therefore demanded evocative if not provoking language. For nothing is guaranteed to dam God's grace more effectively than a wrong attitude, particularly one inspired by pious bigotry.

This was, I believe, in the mind of Jesus when he said: 'The man who has will always be given more, but the man who has not will forfeit even what he has' (Luke 19.26, NEB). Superficially nothing could be more unjust, but in fact such an outcome is intrinsically inescapable. For the two men represent extremes in attitudes to life. One possesses because he knows how to receive; he will, said

Jesus, always be *given* more. We have already noticed that the best things in life – sometimes called spiritual values – cannot be deserved or earned. They are gifts, free, gratis, unmerited. Ask any man or woman in love. Talk – later of course – to a man under the spell of a Beethoven sonata; or to a hospital patient recovering from a major operation; or to a sufferer from insomnia after his first good night's sleep for months. The best things in life *are* free. They cannot be accumulated any more than sunshine can be trapped by pulling the curtains or a gentle breeze stored in a bag. They can only be received. And our capacity to receive is determined by our attitude to the whole of life. This indicates why the grace of God, the spiritual energy that nourishes a man's inner resources and gives him resilience in the face of every adversity, is available to people far beyond the confines of organized religion. It is readily available to everyone prepared to receive it. If the attitude or outlook is right, it flows without respect of persons or labels or even morality. The last word is dangerous because it lends itself to grave misunderstanding, but the idea it represents is important to our discussion. Some of us seek to acquire moral status in the same way that the miser seeks money. We secretly tot up our achievements not only to wallow in feelings of smugness and spiritual superiority, but to prove to God that we deserve his blessing. Far from sincerely saying, 'We are servants and deserve no credit; we have only done our duty' (Luke 17.10, NEB), we tend to congratulate God on having such 'unworthy' servants as ourselves. Beyond our perception, we bargain with God, submitting a catalogue of our good works as evidence that he is obligated to grant us public success as distinct from the success that belongs essentially to our secret life. We might use the right words of prayer and subscribe to an evangelical system of theology, but our spirit (another name for attitude) is wrong and blocks the grace of God. There are, on the other hand, people like the young secularists I have described, who, along with the tax-gatherers and harlots, have moral standards of which we disapprove, but whose attitude to life bespeaks love, forgiveness, tenderness, acceptance, strong gentleness, and is utterly free of the censoriousness that sometimes characterizes zealous evangelists like ourselves. In saying this, I have no wish to condone lower moral standards or to suggest that worldly sinners are better (or worse for that matter) than evangelical puritans. The only point I want to make is that basic attitudes to life, not unyielding doctrinal beliefs, open the sluice gates of God's grace and enable individuals, prepared to receive, to tap or unconsciously to appropriate the riches of spiritual power. This secret nourishing of the soul often happens beyond a man's immediate knowing for the same reason that he enjoys good health without trying. Unconsciously he obeys the laws of physical health – laws he barely knows about, let alone deliberately tries to keep – with the result that he remains fit and even improves his general condition. Far from worrying about his health, he unthinkingly maintains it by living vigorously in harmony with its essential requirements. Indeed, if he started to pay overmuch attention to it, he might finish up a hypochondriac and a physical wreck. In the same sort of way, many professed disbelievers in God, people who give little or no thought to their spirituality, fulfil by their very attitude to life the laws of spiritual health – laws that govern life within the kingdom of God – with the result that they grow in grace and assimilate the power released to any man who shares, knowingly or not, the perspective of Christ.

Thousands of young rebels against institutional religion are, I believe, fortified in their compassionate concern for the underprivileged by the self-same resources that are available to me and evangelicals like me. Just as they know God by some other name, so they receive his grace in ways other than those especially advocated by the church. He is the unrealized inspiration of so much youthful idealism and altruism, the gentle pressure towards sacrificial caring that multitudes of young people experience, the glow of fulfilment that comes to them as they lose themselves in service for others. He works secretly and silently, unconcerned about the names and terms men use to talk about the meaning of life and their exploration of truth. We evangelicals believe with the authority of our own experience that the Carpenter of Nazareth reveals most directly and fully the mystery of the Godhead. But the Spirit of truth, whom Jesus said the Father would send in his name, is abroad in the world and ministering, as we have seen Jesus did in the flesh, to man's needs *anonymously*.

Concluding his book *The Quest of the Historical Jesus*, Albert Schweitzer wrote the now famous words:

*He comes to us as one unknown*, without a name, as of old by the lake-side he came to those who knew him not. He speaks to us the same word, 'Follow thou me', and sets us to the task which he has to fulfill in our time. He commands. And to those who obey him, whether they be wise or simple, he will reveal himself in the toils, the conflicts, the sufferings which they shall pass through in his fellowship, and, as an ineffable mystery, they shall learn in their own experience who he is (my italics).[1]

He still comes as one unknown, speaking similar words, and to those who follow – live in his spirit, share his perspective, support his loyalties – he will just as assuredly reveal himself in their own experience, as the Way, the Truth, and the Life.

This is forcibly illustrated to my mind by what we call the parable of the sheep and the goats (Matt. 25.31-46). Jesus was talking about judgment. He said of the 'blessed' that when he was hungry and thirsty they gave him food and drink, when a stranger they took him in, when naked they clothed him, when ill they helped him, when in prison they visited him. Their only reaction was one of incredulity. They had no recollection of having done such things. Jesus explained: 'I tell you this: anything you did for one of my brothers here, however humble, you did for me' (v. 40). In serving them they had unconsciously served him. In meeting human need they had unknowingly ministered to him. Their one aim had been to alleviate human suffering, but at the same time they had advanced the cause of Christ and won his approval, meaning surely his support. For is it conceivable that the living Lord would accept their service for others as though it were offered to himself without seeking to replenish their inner resources; making readily available to them what we Christians call the grace of God?

Such grace flows along many channels. Some of them, well tried and unfailing, belong to the ministry of the church and continue to meet the needs of countless worshippers. Others of them are more surprising or unexpected and rarely receive the acknowledgment they deserve. Not a few get choked with the weeds of human selfishness which reduce the flow to a trickle. But God uses them all and does not restrict their effectiveness merely because some of us insist upon thinking of any of them in only

[1] A. & C. Black 1954, p. 401.

secular or even God-denying terms.

We can do no better than conclude this chapter with another quotation from Paul Tillich's *The Shaking of the Foundations*. He wrote:

Grace strikes us when we are in great pain and restlessness. It strikes us when we walk through the dark valley of a meaningless and empty life. It strikes us when we feel that our separation is deeper than usual because we have violated another life, a life which we loved, or from which we were estranged. It strikes us when our disgust for our own being, our indifference, our weakness, our hostility, and our lack of direction and composure have become intolerable to us. It strikes us when, year after year, the longed-for perfection of life does not appear, when the old compulsions reign within us as they have for decades, when despair destroys all joy and courage. Sometimes at that moment a wave of light breaks into our darkness, and it is as though a voice were saying: 'You are accepted. *You are accepted*, accepted by that which is greater than you, and the name of which you do not know. Do not ask for the name now; perhaps you will find it later. Do not try to do anything now; perhaps later you will do much. Do not seek for anything now; do not perform anything; do not intend anything. Simply accept the fact that you are accepted!' If that happens to us, we experience grace.[1]

[1] SCM Press 1949; Pelican Books, p. 163.

# IO

# *God is Fulfilment*

In this chapter I want to explain what I mean by claiming that God is known by another name in such experiences as forgiveness, freedom from fear, and self-fulfilment. The terms are unimportant, and probably convey restricted meanings anyway, but they point to what I have previously called Reality, meaning the ground of our being, depth, and other expressions of authenticity for us. Let me start with a true life incident. A professional social worker was telling me about a remarkable woman she met regularly in the course of her rounds. This woman, an incurable cripple, was virtually never free from pain, completely housebound and dependent upon daily visits from the district nurse, incapable of doing most things for herself, and physically infirm to the point of absolute immobility unless helped by somebody else. She was placed in her commode every morning and remained there until put back to bed at night at a time convenient to the caller. Unable to engage in occupational therapy of any kind, she simply sat all day, alone and isolated. What impressed the social worker was the woman's cheerfulness, her positive attitude to life. She radiated optimism and serenity. To be in her presence was to feel uplifted. Her spirit was a triumphant denial of the pathetic situation in which she lived. The social worker, not given to overstatement or romanticizing, the very opposite, said that this woman never complained or talked about her trials. She was almost too good to be true; yet she was true, and proved herself so year after year. I learned that she had no conscious faith in God, received no ministrations of any kind from the church, and appeared to be indifferent to such matters. She had never been a churchgoer in her adult life and had never felt that way disposed. As with my youthful secularists, God was for her a closed book, an unnecessary luxury for people that way inclined.

The social worker was convinced that the secret of this woman's outstanding sanctity was her belief that life itself was on the side of forgiveness; that all the forces and energies of life were somehow harnessed to healing and redemptive ends. Being a simple woman, she never thought in such terms herself, but everything about her suggested that this was her philosophy. She was certainly a 'secular saint'. Perhaps Martin Luther King was giving voice to the same sort of conviction when he testified:

God has been profoundly real to me in recent years. In the midst of lonely days and dreary nights I have heard an inner voice saying, 'Lo, I will be with you'. When the chains of fear and the manacles of frustration have all but stymied my efforts, I have felt the power of God transforming the fatigue of despair into the buoyancy of hope. *I am convinced that the universe is under the control of a loving purpose, and that in the struggle for righteousness man has cosmic companionship. Behind the harsh appearances of the world there is a benign power* (my italics).[1]

It was Robert Louis Stevenson, himself no stranger to chronic and incurable suffering, who said, 'I believe in the ultimate decency of things'; and thereby from within his Christian faith pointed, it seems to me, to the same truth that anchored the crippled woman. She did not, of course, believe in any formal or cut-and-dried manner; her spirit or outlook was the expression of certain intuitive assumptions, things she took for granted, hammered out on the anvil of experience and woven into the very fabric of her being. Basic to them all was this certitude that, as the social worker put it, life itself was on the side of forgiveness. I inquired of the social worker whether such words meant to her what I mean when I talk about the love of God. Without hesitation she confirmed that this was so. Then are we not justified in concluding that God's love, though never remotely recognized as such, can still be known in the sort of ways that this woman's experience typifies? To think otherwise is to claim that God is forever outside the experience of 'secular saints', debarred from their life and situation by considerations of theological orthodoxy. Nothing could be more out of harmony with the total view of the New Testament.

In believing that the forces and energies of life were somehow harnessed to healing and redemptive ends, the woman was not

[1] *Strength to Love*, Collins, Fontana Books 1969, p. 154.

seeking to relieve her own distress by escaping into a fantasy world of false hope. Realizing long ago that nothing basic could be done about her physical condition, she accepted the fact and was reconciled to it. Yet she remained so convinced that life was fundamentally benevolent that nothing could get her down. At the very centre of life there was, she believed, a redemptive principle ceaselessly at work. She did not think of it in personal terms as Christians think of God. She did not imagine for one moment that it guaranteed for her either release from her trials or preferential treatment over other sufferers. It represented help *in* adversity more than freedom *from* it. She knew that life must go on, whatever happened, but it did so, she felt, rather like a stream of vitality and creative power, ministering by the very nature of things to human need. A similar conviction was expressed by Dr Norman Pittenger in his book *Love Looks Deep*:

Implicit in the common experience of promise-making [he wrote] is the conviction – very often and most obviously implicit or unspoken, sometimes denied in words by those who claim to see no possible significance in 'this scheme of things entire' – that we live in a world which mysteriously possesses an ultimate meaning, in relation to which the enterprise of making promises has point and value. Perhaps this is one of the clearest instances of the often unspoken and sometimes denied human assurance that *God is* – not necessarily the 'god' of any religious faith, but certainly the divine reality who is the final structure and the ultimate dynamic in all things.[1]

Now this was, I believe, the central axiom upon which Jesus based his life and thought. It fed his faith in the face of adversity, bewilderment and doubt; it guarded his peace in situations of turmoil and tension. Confronted by the prospect of his own crucifixion, and facing daily the anguish that inevitably preceded it, he remained firm in his conviction that ultimately love would triumph and truth be vindicated. Appearances often suggested otherwise, not least to his disciples who finally forsook him when he needed them most; and Jesus himself was almost overwhelmed, shouting from the cross his protest against God's apparent indifference. But he remained certain that no matter how impenetrable the darkness final victory was assured. In the light of that conviction, even his execution was really defeat triumphant, the out-

[1] A. R. Mowbray and Co. 1969, p. 23.

working of love's conquest of evil, a fact confirmed and illustrated by the resurrection. Once this truth took hold of the disciples they were irresistible and fearless in propagating its message, sharing with anyone prepared to listen the news that at the heart of the cosmos was a loving heart, revealed in the life, death and resurrection of Jesus Christ, a love that would not let men go or rest until its redemptive purposes were fulfilled. No wonder they believed that evil had shot its bolt and death lost its sting. No wonder they sang in tribulation and maintained in every experience what someone described as 'apostolic optimism', surely the same sort of optimism that characterized the crippled woman in her lonely helplessness. Her intuitive faith in life's fundamental benevolence was and is identical in *experience* to the certitude that God's love for the world is ultimately undefeatable. At one time, knowing that she was a stranger to evangelical theology, I would have wanted to talk to her about the love of God, the sacrifice of Christ, his conquest of death, and his living presence in the life of every believer. Now I am inclined to think that such a woman knows God's love and shares Christ's victory to such an extent that she is able to give me greater understanding of my theology and interpret for me another way in which truth – the many-sided truth of infinite love – is both revealed and apprehended. She does not need God; she knows him already by some other name.

The name varies according to background and circumstances. I remember talking to the son of Salvation Army officer parents. A graduate, he came to work at Regent Hall for his long summer vacation before commencing post-graduate studies. He wore Salvation Army uniform and from the standpoint of compassionate service was a paragon Salvationist; indeed, in my twenty-odd years of officership I have met few individuals more dedicated or involved in human need. He told me quite frankly that my evangelical theology only bewildered him. For a number of years, notably in his adolescence, he had tried out of a sense of loyalty to fit his spiritual experience into the thought-patterns of the Salvation Army, but this finally had proved impossible and a source of growing tension. Yet there was no doubt in my mind, or his, about the reality of his spiritual experience; it explained his presence at Regent Hall for service among young drifters, drug abusers and the like, and caused him, incidentally, to postpone his post-graduate studies for two years so that, at no little cost to himself in numerous ways, he could remain with us. But that experience was not helped or adequately defined by his trying to reconcile it to orthodox statements of belief. 'When you talk about the love of God,' he said, 'I don't really understand what you mean. I think you're referring to the experience I prefer to call freedom from fear.' Those three words represented the nearest approximation he could think of to the reality he knew but found impossible to verbalize.

*Freedom from fear!* This was utterly different from stoicism, the attitude to life that suggests more passivity than participation. Still less was it related to the apparent fearlessness that grits its teeth and screws up its nerves in an attempt to hide its inherent cowardice. My young colleague was talking about a spiritual quality that expressed his groping yet deepening conviction that the key to man's inner conflict was his capacity to love; that freedom from fear was an exercise in loving, not, mark you, of God, but of man the neighbour. You will not be surprised to learn that his words reminded me of the promise of Jesus: 'you shall know the truth, and the truth will set you free ... If then the Son sets you free, you will indeed be free' (John 8.32, 36, NEB); and of the comment found in the first letter of John:

God is love; he who dwells in love is dwelling in God, and God in him. This is for us the perfection of love, to have confidence on the day of judgment, and this we can have because even in this world we are as he is. There is no room for fear in love; perfect love banishes fear.

(I John, 4.17-18, NEB).

The young man, realizing that fear, like fire, was a wonderful servant but a terrible master, knew the difference between fear and terror. It was the latter that was being expurgated from his life through, it seemed to me, his unconscious discovery of God's love on a deeper level in caring relationships with all sorts of moral and social cripples. But he disagreed, not without a measure of exasperation. 'Why drag God into it?' he asked; 'I'm not sure what the name means, and anyway, we're talking about my experience, not your theology.'

What could not be denied was that his emphasis – freedom from fear – made immediate sense to the youngsters among whom he lived and worked. They wanted nothing to do with God as taught by the church, and turned impatiently away at the very suggestion that they did, but fear was their constant companion. Their world was full of it, creating phobias, lies, deceit, panic, fantasies, anxiety, hate, exploitation, lack of confidence, and countless other barriers to personal integration and well-being. Freedom from fear! Now this was what they really wanted – to explore the nature and possibility of such an experience; to discover something of its meaning in relationships of loving mutuality; to find a measure of freedom from the terror of silent loneliness, the dread of rejection, the realization of folly and futility. Is there a more exciting prospect for any of us, orthodox Christian or not? I had always known that perfect love casts out fear, and had believed that such love was most readily available to us, perhaps only so, as we exercised faith in Christ, knelt in surrender at the cross and perceived there the true nature of God's love. But now I was compelled to recognize that freedom from fear was possible without conscious faith in God or concern about transcendental relationships of any kind. To my mind the evidence was irrefutable, not just because of one person's experience, but because of the growing number of young people I met who denied belief in God as such but clearly enjoyed the fruits of his presence in their lives. It seemed to me that while I was concerned about the *Cause*, which I called God, they were preoccupied with the *consequences* of what I believed to be his activity. They neither realized nor cared that God was the initiator. All that mattered to them was their greater understanding of the consequences, thought of by themselves, of course, as simply life's experiences. But can Cause and consequences ever be separated? And is it possible to know the latter without in some way being in touch with the former? To be more explicit, can we separate God by our theological terms from the consequences he causes in our lives? Indeed, to go a step further, can God be known not only as Cause but as Consequence, a different matter from the belief that he is present *in* consequence? There is, I believe, a vital distinction, one that if valid enables us to drop as we desire the word G-O-D altogether and concentrate on those points of human experience that reveal, so Christians believe, the consequences of God's ceaseless redemptive activity.

When some of my young friends talked about their progressive understanding of freedom from fear, talked about it with the same joyful assurance that marked the testimonies of early day Salvation Army converts, I was convinced that they were in touch with the Reality whom I call God; and that he was leading them into the self-same areas of truth most illuminated for me by conscious fellowship with Jesus Christ. Their number was small and certainly they were not typical of young people in the Salvation Army or – I imagine – the church generally. This is not important. What most concerns me is the ready assumption we evangelicals make that such individuals still need to be converted; that they are outside a personal experience of God's love and can only be admitted by their deliberate faith in the saving power of Jesus Christ. I believe that they know God already by other names and terms. They experience the same Love that we symbolize with the letters G O-D, and interpret that experience in ways meaningful to themselves. The more orthodox among us obviously prefer the old terminology and are justified in continuing to use it; but not, I hasten to add, if we think that somehow it thereby guarantees for us a monopoly of truth and makes possession of our spiritual riches entirely contingent upon the acceptance and use of their traditional definitions.

These and related themes were the basis for informal discussion which often grew out of our spontaneous consideration with all sorts of people of what life was all about; the things that concern us most. We all wanted to live to the full, to discover what Jesus called life more abundant, which was, we decided, identical in experience to what some of our number meant when they talked about self-fulfilment. They argued that organized or institutional religion often made this more unlikely for the believer, adding to his burdens by imposing impossible moral standards, with the guilt, dejection, and weariness that inevitably go with them. There's no doubt that religion represents for many people insufferable and seemingly endless obligations that can never be met. It demands that they pray (in itself a major problem for some), love everybody, turn the other cheek, attend church, read the Bible, support good causes, bear their witness to all and sundry (another source of acute nervous tension for the ultra-conscientious), visit the sick, comfort the sad; the list is infinite. And when they fail they feel more crushed and worthless, more condemned and rejected, more futile and useless. Yet they pick themselves up and again set out on the same frustrating round of hope, defeat, guilt, self-despising, confession, and precarious hope reborn, which, alas, proves to be the prelude to nothing more than the same old vicious circle. Obviously this is contrary either to God's intentions or to the experience of many devout members of the church, but it represents the only sort of personal religion that too many people know. Far from aiding their fulfilment as real persons, it keeps them in a state of immaturity; stunted, resentful, ridden with guilt and never more than partially alive.

One of the basic explanations of this tragic situation is a common tendency to identify religion with morality; people interpret religion as nothing more than the stern obligation to fulfil the letter of the moral law. They imagine that evidence of their goodness (meaning their good works) alone endears them to God and somehow qualifies them to receive his blessing. But the inescapable corollary is also uppermost in their minds – that to fail in good works, to fail, in fact, in anything at all, is to displease God and to warrant nothing but his enmity. They imagine themselves as unfit to be loved by God and think of life as an unequal struggle to prove otherwise. If only they would stop trying to be religious, meaning for them stop measuring religious faith in terms of moral achievement only. But they stumble along the high road of their moral imperatives and think of God as not unlike a revered schoolmaster making demands forever beyond the capacity of his pupils who feel wretched when they fail him.

The essential meaning of religion is relationships, not righteousness. It goes without saying, of course, that the right sort of relationship between God and man issues in righteous living, or at least works towards that end, but God's relationship with man is dependent upon, let me reiterate, more our basic attitudes than our moral attainments. What else is the meaning of the parable of the Pharisee and the publican (Luke 18.9-14)? The Pharisee's moral attainments were impressive enough, but his basic attitude to God, to religion and life, was one of self-righteousness, the spirit that separates from God and self. The publican, on the other hand, despite his confessed unworthiness, had the attitude that enabled him to receive (not attempt to win) the help he sought and needed from God. He accepted that he was accepted, and thereby, whether he understood the reason for it or not, knew the peace of self-acceptance. I am not playing with words. Self-acceptance is a gift beyond price and essential to self-fulfilment. It points to the reason why so many of us are frustrated, weary of trying, and less fulfilled than some of our non-religious friends and neighbours. Perhaps it is that we fail to perceive not only the essential nature of religion, but also the reason for our own inner restlessness. We are creatures longing for fulfilment, the end for which we were made and the goal to which we all seek to journey.

Now Christians believe that the creator of all life is God who therefore knows the secret of fulfilment; that he has revealed that secret in numerous ways, ways that men have formulated into laws and philosophies, but that supremely his secret has been made known in the life, death and resurrection of Jesus Christ. There is no denying that multitudes of people, including our young drifters, drug abusers, flower children and many others, disagree, but this does not alter the fact that the common denominator that binds us all together is our search for personal fulfilment. How can it be obtained? What is it we are seeking to fulfil anyway – a significant question that compels us immediately to inquire into the total nature and meaning of man? For if man is a trinity of body, mind and spirit, then clearly he will never find fulfilment if he thinks of himself only in physical and material terms, and his temporal world as devoid of spiritual meaning. From this position of argument, Dr Norman Pittenger made the observation:

Ultimately, the only love, which will satisfy man is God's love, which is to say, God himself. 'Thou hast made us as moving towards thee, O God,' said St Augustine, 'and our heart is in disquietude until it finds its satisfaction and rest in thee.'[1]

I agree. But what of those who disbelieve in God? Are they therefore debarred from the experience of knowing his love and finding fulfilment in it? Not so, as Dr Pittenger went on to make clear:

But because we are human, time-and-space-bound creatures, God has provided for us a surrogate of himself as love. That surrogate, or instru-

[1] *Love Looks Deep*, pp. 58-9.

mental representative, is another of our own kind. So, in loving other men, we come to share in the divine love itself. We learn to love God, but first because we have loved him in his creation. Then we can love him in and for himself; yet never in total separation from his creation, for the creation can never be separated from him. The central Christian affirmation that God was in Christ, truly dwelling and working in genuine human life, is the sheet-anchor for this truth ... And to love God, in and through and with his creation, in and through and with another human being in that creation, is the most profound and complete fulfilment to which man can attain. It is *life*, in the richest meaning of that word – and any lover knows what I am talking about even if he has never put it in just such words.[1]

Fulfilment as God intended it is possible without conscious faith in him so long as the requirements of love are satisfied. The trouble is that those requirements are not self-evident, far from it, a fact made painfully obvious by, for instance, considerations of sexuality. I have already mentioned that some of the young people with whom we were involved, members of the Rink club and the flower children's club, thought of love exclusively in terms of physical love-making. For them sex was the union of two bodies, an act providing pleasurable physical sensations, but leaving the participants strangely unsatisfied, a pathetic symbol of their general frustration. They failed to see that neither their mutual desire to exploit (or willingness to be exploited) nor their mutual fidelity for as long as that particular relationship lasted was sufficient to overcome the germs of self-destruction within their experience of sex. They reduced persons to things; practised self-gratification in the name of love; and satisfied their hunger but never their appetite. The more they indulged, the greater their frustration. Finally sex merely confirmed their suspicion that life always promised mountains and delivered mole-hills. They were back in square one – seeking self-fulfilment without satisfying the essential requirements of love.

Most of us do the same in relationships of every type, imposing ourselves, manipulating other people, exploiting their affection, taking advantage of their kindness, asserting ourselves at the cost of another's diminution, and furthering self-interest under the guise of self-giving. The result is our own disappointment, disintegration, maladjustment, and sickness of soul. Frustration is the opposite of fulfilment and – as previously intimated – is overcome

[1] ibid.

more by direction of life than doctrinal belief. This is not to underestimate the importance of doctrinal belief, which obviously expresses itself in direction of life, sometimes pathetically so, but it is to make a necessary emphasis, one that many young idealists are working out without conscious reference to God or orthodox Christianity at all. They are finding personal fulfilment in learning what it means to love, not only within the context of sexuality, but in relationships generally. They are discovering that sin is unloving intention: taking, bullying, coercing, misleading, extorting, pressurizing, sometimes in insidiously 'affectionate' ways; it is cynicism, patronage, contempt, insensitivity, indifference, sarcasm, laughter at another's expense, expediency, charm without commitment, praise without principle, insincere protest. In the triumphs and travails of life, its light and shade, pleasure and pain, they are sharpening their insight into self-knowledge, exploring the implications of self-acceptance, and moving ever deeper into the inexhaustible riches of self-fulfilment. As they do so, they unconsciously reflect the mind of Christ and share progressively the joy that his coming into the world released.

# II

# *Secular Spirituality*

At the age of eighty-eight and after a life-time of service to the church, including more than thirty years as Dean of St Paul's, Dr W. R. Matthews confessed:

> I am glad that there was never a serious proposal that I should be a bishop for more than one reason; but chief among them is the consciousness that, although I persevered in prayer, I have never advanced far in the art. [1]

His experience of prayer is only too typical, though most of us hardly persevere. We give up, bored and bewildered. More serious still, we feel guilty, deficient of spirituality and rightly the object of God's disapproval. In my Salvation Army officership, I have come across far more unhappiness caused by prayer and its problems than by drunkenness and adultery. Some of the finest Christians I have known have confided in me their wretchedness at not being able to pray. They have tried with commendable tenacity, observing quiet times, adhering to traditional patterns of devotion, using well-proven spiritual aids, and seeking with faith and love to make their worship real; but the result has been disastrous. At least that is how they have felt about it.

The discipline has been fruitless for as long as they can remember. They have tried numerous techniques, sought the aid of prayer manuals, including such modern masterpieces as Michel Quoist's *Prayers of Life*,[2] turned to every new translation of the

---

[1] *Memories and Meanings*, Hodder & Stoughton 1969, p. 64.
[2] M. H. Gill, 1965; see also Douglas Rhymes, *Prayer in the Secular City*, Lutterworth 1967; Malcolm Boyd, *Book of Days*, Heinemann and SCM Press 1968; Carl Burke, *Treat Me Cool, Lord*, Collins, Fontana Books 1969.

Bible in the hope of discovering the secret of prayer for themselves, kept devotional diaries, prayed audibly in private, written
letters of prayerful aspiration, and seized upon every promise of
escaping the nagging suspicion that prayer was for them a waste
of time. Finally, they have given up the practice of prayer while
continuing to offer lip-service to its importance.

This inconsistency has been the very opposite of hypocrisy or
pious deceit. They have simply concluded that prayer, though
obviously important, is not for them, for reasons detrimental to
themselves. Their attitude has been one of self-criticism, not criticism of prayer as taught by the church and practised by devout
Christians for two thousand years. I want to emphasize that their
difficulties have been not only wandering thoughts and recalcitrant
feelings, though in all conscience these have been problematical
enough, but their whole experience of prayer has been unsatis-
factory; more demoralizing than inspiring, and artificial than real.

All too often such people are urged to continue, to ignore their
feelings and to exercise more faith. The impression is given –
probably not deliberately – that they are wholly to blame and
that once they learn the technique of prayer everything, including their suspicions of futility, will fall into rightful place. There
is, of course, an element of truth in such counsel, for some of us
are too easily discouraged or, more likely still, imagine that prayer
is comfort before discipline. But it also could be that our concept of prayer is too narrow, too conditioned by church-centred
emphases and the idea of separation from the hurly-burly of life.
There are people who continue to think of prayer as little more
than kneeling down, closing their eyes and putting their hands
together; rather after the fashion of kneeling at mother's knee in
childhood. They conceive of prayer as a refuge, a place to which
to escape from harsh reality or from which to venture into a
bleak world. For them, often the victims of false or unbalanced
teaching, prayer is a time of preparation for living and a conva-
lescence for its wounds; as though the pray-er spent time in God's
presence at the beginning of the day, rushed out into an alien
world to fulfil his obligations, and then gratefully at the first
opportunity scurried back to God for another devotional interlude.

Prayer is life, an exercise in real encounter and sensitive involvement. Such words, I realize, are over-worked, but they have no

satisfactory substitutes. Without encounter and involvement there is no vital praying, a truth pointing to the fact that prayer requires loving identification more than physical participation; the monk in his cell, for instance, sensitive and compassionate, is capable of projecting himself imaginatively into a situation of prayerful concern. For prayer is not only or even primarily something we *do*; it is fundamentally something we *are*, whatever our circumstances. And this means that though often we rightly stop thinking about God, we never stop praying. In their pursuit of personal holiness, some evangelicals, sincere and dedicated people, have aspired constantly to think of God. They have tried to do their work with one eye on him, and felt guilty when this has rightly proved to be impossible. Motivated by religious belief, they have lived irreligiously by not giving themselves wholly or adequately to their daily work. What could be more irreligious, for example, than a pious shop assistant giving more thought to God than to her waiting customers; or a devout fireman fighting the flames with less thought for the people trapped on the top floor than for his morning Bible-reading. The Christian surgeon has more than God on his mind as he performs the delicate operation. His religion is expressed as he forgets God and concentrates on his immediate responsibility. He prays as he works, without conscious reference to God at all. The measure of his devoutness is not the extent to which he remembers God, but the thoroughness with which he meets his immediate responsibility. The former Bishop of Woolwich, Dr John Robinson, in *Honest to God*, surely the most vehemently condemned, unread bestseller of all time within evangelical circles, has this to say about prayer:

My own experience is that I am really **pra**ying for people, agonizing with God for them, precisely *as* I meet them and really give my soul to them. It is then if ever, in this incarnational relationship, that deep speaks to deep and the Spirit of God is able to take up our inarticulate groans and turn them into prayer.

He continued:

Perhaps this is the starting-point for a 'non-religious' understanding of prayer. We may begin from the fact that people do give themselves to people. There is nothing 'religious' about this. But to open oneself to another *unconditionally* in love *is* to be with him in the presence of God, and that is the heart of intercession. To pray for another is to expose both oneself and him to the common ground of our being; it is to see one's concern for him in terms of *ultimate* concern, to let God into the relationship ... It may not be specifically religious, it may not be consciously Christian : but it may be a meeting of Christ in that man, because his humanity is accepted 'without any reservation'. The way through to the vision of the Son of man and the knowledge of God, which is the heart of contemplative prayer, is by unconditional love of the neighbour. [1]

Possibly we shall better understand this interpretation of prayer by approaching it from another standpoint altogether. William Temple gave what has become a standard definition of worship :

... to worship is to quicken the conscience by the holiness of God, to feed the mind with the truth of God, to purge the imagination by the beauty of God, to open the heart to the love of God, to devote the will to the purpose of God. All this is gathered up in that emotion which most cleanses us from selfishness because it is the most selfless of all emotions – adoration. [2]

So it is, but not always in those terms or in identical ways suggested by them. We have already noticed that worship of God and worth-ship of people are related, the one expressing the other, consciously and otherwise. This connection was underlined also by John Robinson when he wrote :

The test of worship is how far it makes us *more sensitive* to 'the beyond in our midst', to the Christ in the hungry, the naked, the homeless and the prisoner. Only if we are *more likely* to recognize him there after attending an act of worship is that worship Christian rather than a piece of religiosity in Christian dress. That is what is implied in Jesus' saying that 'the sabbath was made for man, not man for the sabbath'. The whole of our religious observance and church-going must be prepared to submit to its test.[3]

There can be no doubt that true worship of God consciously offered in love and faith expresses itself in caring for our neighbour. Our worship, let it be noted, is not motivated by such a concern; as though, wanting to be more sensitive, more lovingly involved, we engage in worship as preparation for service, our

[1] SCM Press 1963, p. 99. [2] *The Hope of a New World*, SCM Press 1940, p. 30.
[3] *Honest to God*, p. 90.

real business. We worship God for his own loving sake; we escape our habitual self-centredness in self-forgetful adoration and thanksgiving. Our aim is to give, not get; and to avoid the insidious danger of using worship as a pious means to a selfish end. Any subsequent caring is the spontaneous by-product of soul vitality, vitality not directly sought but made inevitable by true worship of God. In other words, the reality and depth of our worship is the degree and spirit of our caring; of our self-giving, our personal relationships, our sensitivity. We love God only to the extent that we love people. We pray for people only to the limit of our commitment to them. If, remembering John Robinson's words, the test of our worship is the nature of our subsequent service to Christ in the hungry, the naked, the homeless and the prisoner, surely such service is simply another expression of the same authentic spirit of worship. It works both ways. Worship is real when men learn to care; and men learn to care when worship is real. For what is worship? Certainly everything suggested by William Temple's definition, but also our response to 'the beyond in our midst'; to the Christ in the needy, using that word 'needy' in its broadest sense. In a previous chapter we noticed how, in the parable of the sheep and the goats, the 'blessed' were totally unaware that when they gave themselves in service to people they were also giving themselves in spirit to the Son of man. The reality of their offering to him was not invalidated by their failure to perceive the spiritual nature of their self-giving. They prayed beyond their knowing and, I believe, worshipped God by living in the spirit of worth-ship, notably towards people in danger of losing sight of their own significance. Worship and prayer are not, I realize, synonymous, but my free interchange is, I think, justifiable within this context if only to emphasize that the religious spirit common to both is capable of numerous expressions, not least in seemingly non-religious situations.

The question is – and I hear it asked repeatedly by orthodox Christians – can the spirit of worth-ship of people be maintained without conscious worship of God? In the books on 'secular prayer' and other considerations of spirituality within secular society, I get the impression that the answer is definitely no. Everyone agrees that the spirit of worship and prayer can be expressed in the manner suggested above; indeed, the unanimous insistence is that without such expressions traditional spiritual exercises are useless and even dangerous. But the assumption is still made that prayer as taught by the church is essential; that we all need time to stand back and re-focus on the eternal perspective, to talk and to listen to God, to look at everyday affairs through the eyes of Jesus. This is undoubtedly true for me and many believers like me, but clearly not for everybody in those terms. Life itself illustrates that Christian prayer as traditionally practised is not indispensable to Christian caring. I repeat, it is for me. But I know people who are positively hindered by their attempts to conform to customary patterns of prayer. They have felt burdened by the obligation to pray, the daily commitment that has added to their troubles and become a source of anxiety and guilt. Some of them, by giving up prayer as taught by the church, have discovered to their own surprise a new reality in their personal religion. Before meeting such people, and sharing with them unhurriedly some of their problems of faith, I would have argued that prayer as most orthodox believers understand it was essential to mature spirituality, but their experience has compelled me to think otherwise. One of them assures me that he only really began to live, to know peace of mind, when some eight years ago, after struggling for years to cultivate a devotional life in traditional ways, he abandoned the daily discipline of prayer unreservedly and has not thought in such terms since. Indeed, the only time he consciously tries to pray at all is congregationally in church on Sundays, and this, he insists, is for him unreal and unhelpful. It is surely significant that such individuals, far from losing their faith in God, have found what I can only describe as 'rest to their soul'; the certitude that true spirituality is more direction in daily living than devotion in private praying. I am not suggesting that their thinking about prayer supersedes the more customary ideas that still make good sense for multitudes of Christians. Neither am I wishing to imply that their way is superior and should be followed by everybody. My only concern is to illustrate that our traditional concept of spirituality is too narrow, too exclusive, and perhaps too intolerant of new dimensions. God is, I believe, revealing himself to secular men in new ways, ways proven by the spirituality they encourage. To turn our backs upon them is possibly to restrict God's revelation and to risk unnecessary spiritual impoverishment.

Equally serious, it is further to alienate a growing number of individuals who fundamentally share our spirituality, but not our ideas about it.

We all agree that prayer, like worship, is more than a devotional technique, an exercise in ritualistic piety. Basically, prayer is desire; and seeing that we never stop desiring, even in our sleep, we never stop praying. When the apostle Paul exhorts us to 'pray without ceasing', an aim not restricted to the cloistered life, he is clearly not calling us to spend every waking hour on our knees, eyes turned heavenward. He is referring to constancy in prayerful aspiration, another name for desire. Pious words cannot be a substitute for healthy (holy) desire or a camouflage for evil intent; they merely make spoken prayer an indulgence in devout pretentiousness. The trouble is that by the very nature of things bad desires are answered. But so are the good. For when our desires are in harmony with the evaluations of Christ we are desiring in his name, according to his nature. This indicates how secular man unconsciously engages in Christian prayer. His desires, revealing both insight into his own total nature and the spirit of worth-ship he feels for other people, reflect beyond his knowing the mind of Christ, the perspective that Jesus incarnated and taught. He prays with his desires which express themselves in words, groans, silent longings or practical service. And who is to say which is more prayerful – desire that expresses itself on its knees in sustained intercession or with its sleeves rolled up in fetching and carrying or in fostering loving relationships or in giving itself in single-minded listening? Each is evidence of concern, of caring, and prompted by the same spirit of commitment, the identical desire to love. One expression is not inherently spiritually superior to the others, despite the common assumption that only when loving desire is translated into spoken piety is true prayer being uttered. Some of us still cling to the old concepts of sacred and secular, of religion being something we do apart from the main stream of life. We fail to see that the impulse to love and every aspiration towards that end is another expression of the very spirit of prayer – holy desire.

Now this desire is clearly not dependent upon the practice of orthodox prayer. People of all religious faiths, and of none, with no allegiance to institutional religion at all, have it. One of the arguments of this book is that despite the spread of secularization and secularism more and more individuals are living according to Christian insight and evaluations. This applies particularly to the young. They are consumed with holy desire, though the very idea would sicken them. Their motivation, as we have seen, is not God, religion or piety of any kind. They are secularists, suspicious of spirituality and contemptuous of the church. But their basic desires are centred in the welfare of society, the worth-ship of people. They are critical of institutional religion for the very reason, among others, that it appears to pray when bold action is urgently demanded to alleviate human need. Paradoxically, secular man is turning from the church because he sees – or thinks he sees – too little evidence that she is characterized by the right sort of desire or concern. He is joining other organizations, or forming new ones, to do what he believes should be the business of the church. And his desire to meet human need is not only concerned with the physical and material. He seeks to minister to man as a total personality, recognizing that people's needs often belong to the mystery of their inner life.

Some Christians believe – I think rightly so – that secular man's new sensitivity and willingness to serve is but evidence that God the Holy Spirit is at work. Far from being excluded by secular society's indifference and disbelief, he is the author of every noble impulse, the light that lightens every man who comes into the world. The secularist disagrees, but this does not alter the fact or nature of his desires which, I believe, constitute his prayers. As with every man, Christian or otherwise, his desires alone determine the measure of his spirituality. It is sometimes secular only in name. For many a person desires in the spirit of Christ without conscious reference to him.

The significant point is that all desire, like prayer deliberately directed to God, is answered according to its intensity. The single-minded achieve the best results. Jesus said: 'Again I tell you this: If two of you agree on earth about any request you have to make, that request will be granted by my heavenly Father' (Matt. 18. 19, NEB). The request is granted, it seems to me, by the depth of the agreement, not the words of petition that express it. Jesus was talking about a law of life that operates in every situation. Let a young couple, for instance, really agree about anything; make it their first loyalty; bend their united resources to obtain it; work and save for it with slavish devotion, and they will get it – house, car, growing bank balance, whatever. Their 'receiving' will be determined by the extent of their agreeing, their united desiring. The law operates whether they formally pray or not, think of God or not. It explains why we *are* what we *desire*; no more or less.

Now if, as some spiritual teachers insist, prayer from one standpoint is the fulfilment of law on a higher plane, it follows that when these laws are fulfilled, fulfilled by saint or sinner, believer or secularist, deliberately or fortuitously, then prayer is answered. And if prayer is desire, the things we really want and seek, then our desires are answered, our united requests granted, according to the nature and intensity of our aspirations, perhaps more usually called simply our aims in life. Edwin Muir, the poet, put his finger on this same truth when he wrote in his autobiography : 'I think that if any of us examines his life he will find that most good has come to him from a few loyalties.' [1] Just so. And what are these 'few loyalties' but our predominant desires, the nature of which alone fixes our character and regulates our prayers.

In the light of the above, orthodox Christians might well ask to what extent prayer and spirituality are necessary at all. They know that prayer, though undoubtedly expressing their desires, is also the anvil on which their desires are fashioned and brought into line with the mind of Christ. How is it possible for disbelievers in God and individuals who never consciously pray to maintain the spirit of holy desire? No one denies that many people – and I believe a growing number – have either stopped praying or never started observing times for prayer, have discontinued or never commenced the practice of private devotions, but significantly often beyond their own awareness they have still observed the rhythm of worship and work, of isolation and involvement, of vision and obedience, taking in strength and giving out virtue. In every situation they have sought to be real persons. This, in fact, has been their main emphasis and aim – to *be* rather than to *do*. Some of us, including strictly orthodox pray-ers, have not always been so wise. Anxious to keep up with the quickening pace of contemporary life, and perhaps seeking frantically to

[1] *An Autobiography*, Methuen 1965, p. 281.

justify the existence of the church, we have become – or are in danger of becoming – too busy for the good of our souls. We support programmes of reform, social service, and countless church-centred events, trying to meet growing demands with dwindling numbers, with the result that many of us, clergy and laity alike, are exhausted or moving rapidly in that direction. The church should be involved, as this book has stated categorically and implied time after time, but the essential emphasis should be on *being* or the cultivation of spirituality. Put like that, the impression might be given that I am really pleading for more activity of a spiritual or devotional nature – more prayer meetings, Bible study, discussion groups; in other words, the acceptance of more obligations to do things – pray, study, talk. The very opposite, of course, is the case. I see little hope for true spirituality until we recognize the importance of *being* and concentrate on the inner world – the world of self-discovery, of realizing our personal significance for the right reasons, of accepting ourselves, of engaging in genuine relationships, of responding with integrity to every experience, good and bad, welcomed and feared, knowing that everything can be grist to the mill of fulfilment.

This is something which people are doing inside and outside the church. They perceive that love is the key to life. Some of them progressively discover that love by deliberately exploring it in God with the help of Christ; others learn of it at ever greater depth in self-discovery and in following its dictates in their personal relationships. All of them, convinced that life makes sense only when love is supreme, give their loyalty to the things that harmonize with love, and thereby consciously or unconsciously harness supernatural resources. Whatever the motive, the aim is basically the same, which means that spirituality, synonymous with complete or mature personality, is available to secular man and Christian believer alike.

# 12

# *The Way Forward*

Dr John Robinson, now Dean of Chapel at Trinity College, Cambridge, has repeatedly made it clear that he welcomes every evidence that the church is dying. He argues, and numerous prophetic satellites reflect his views, that the church as presently constituted is discredited and needs to die as a means of her own resurrection. So far so good. But I have a nagging reservation, one related to the often debated question of what is the church. Old structures, we are rightly told, must give way to something more in keeping with the second half of the twentieth century. Now if by old structures is meant organization, administration and inadequate theology I could not agree more; but is the situation quite so simple? In the final analysis church structures are people – ordinary, sincere, devoted members of the local church, the sort of individuals who give their time and money, their love and loyalty, to support what they have been taught to believe is the work of God. Many of them, submitting in faith to traditional indoctrination, have learned only too well to depend upon existing structures. If these structures collapse rather than evolve into something different, they are going to crush countless innocent victims whose primary error was to believe what they were taught by their spiritual leaders. It sounds brave and exciting to talk about destroying church structures, and to take every opportunity of hastening the process, but what about these members of the local church? To smile at their naïvety and pour scorn on their often introverted activities is all too easy, but presumably they are equally important in the eyes of the church – not to mention God – as the multitudes of disbelievers for whom the new structures are urgently required.

I resent the tendency in some quarters to ridicule the local church, described in the Salvation Army as a corps. In my experience the people who comprise such fellowships are the 'salt of the earth'. A minority of them, it's true, are petty and sometimes unworthy in other ways, but they are not typical, which explains why their antics are noteworthy in the first place. To suggest that most church members are a liability, standing in the way of the church's true mission and seeking to preserve old ways rather than face the challenge of the new is a travesty of the usual situation. They *are* the structures of the church, for they implement her policies, sustain her programme, and sacrifice for her cause. Without them there could be no resurrection or anything else. It isn't true either that their efforts are always characterized by futility and near despair. They are too perceptive not to differentiate between activity and progress, and too forward looking to reject all change in the name of loyalty to the past. They are aware of the need to change and usually willing to co-operate to this end but, like their *avant garde* critics, they are more confident of what they have to change *from* than of what they need to change *to*. Unashamedly they are confused, not knowing what to do or what is expected of them by either God or the hierarchy of the church, but their bewilderment is always less pronounced than their spiritual certitude which safeguards their loyalty in this interim of doubt and change. They are living in an overlap of ancient and modern, a common experience for the church at most points of her history. What makes their situation perhaps unique is the speed and immensity of change in today's world. Within this context it is hardly surprising that they are confused and unsure about the next step of their Christian obedience.

Jesus himself lived in an overlap of acute tension between old and new. Yet, radical though he was, he never advocated the immediate replacement of traditional structures. In fact, he supported them, worshipping regularly at both synagogue and temple, and presumably offering his tithe to the glory of God. His support did not condone the malpractices of ecclesiastical administration – as his gesture of cleansing the temple indicated – or imply his unconditional approval. Rather it revealed the strategy of radical evolution in preference to the disruption of revolution. It could be that in these days of convulsive change more extreme measures are required, but if so we are still faced by this problem of the local church. To say that it should be scrapped or at least its decline encouraged, so that a completely new start could be made, is surely to over-simplify and to scatter the sheep in the process of rounding up the strays. Ideas about how best to go forward are bound to vary and will sometimes lead to conflict, even bitterness, but we shall get nowhere by talking glibly about old structures, meaning finally people, being superseded by new structures about which, on our own admission, we know next to nothing.

The basic need is for the local church to become a community of tolerance. There should be more room for people of every possible point of view to work out their ideas and convictions within the united strength of the fellowship but sometimes outside its existing structures. Not everybody is suited to lonely pioneering of uncertain outcome. By temperament and disposition some of us are incapable of stepping beyond the orthodox and usual; we prefer what we know, and feel no need personally for change. On the other hand, we might well *think* radically, but for reasons buried deep in our unconscious remain compliant in our *living*. We recognize the inadequacy of old ways and give wordy support to the policy of bold experimentation, but capitulate when confronted by the first demand of unpopular action. By the very nature of things the majority of us tend to suspect fundamental change anyway. The familiar is meaningful to us, the fountainhead of our knowledge of God and the means of grace that nourish our spiritual lives. Then why, we ask, should we risk losing what is proven in experience for the possibility, no more, of making the church relevant for modern man? Are we, too, not modern and ourselves clear evidence therefore that the church without changing is still able to meet human need? The debate continues, as it should, for the health and well-being of the entire church; its only danger is intolerance, the spirit that makes its own viewpoint the touchstone of truth and becomes acrimonious in the name of holy zeal. This happens so easily when the essential purpose of the church is forgotten; when disagreements degenerate into personal issues, and dogmatism replaces open-mindedness. The answer is not to destroy the local church, to scrap it as reactionary and hopelessly outdated. It is to encourage the development of a community of tolerance; to welcome new ideas, to support bold experimentation within and without existing structures, to foster a spirit of brotherhood in which individuals feel that they can be true to themselves without needing to engage in painful self-justification all the time.

Commenting on the presence in the church of people dissatisfied with the existing set-up, Albert H. van den Heuvel warned:

Two things would be disastrous – to ignore and to integrate. If the group were ignored, they might begin to build their own structure or to disappear, and in both cases they would be lost to the church. But to integrate them is even more dangerous. If people from the group I have described were now called to high posts in the existing structure, they might have to give up their demand for total renewal. There are many who are integrated into the structure and have paid the price – wild geese who have been tamed. But what then? There remains but one thing: for the church to learn how essential is the experiment in their midst, and give money, room, and freedom to the renewers to try out and to formulate the vision of the renewal of the church. It may well be that it will be scornfully noted that the 'old structures' must after all pay for all these experiments. I have never understood what is wrong with that. If the traditional structures are no longer willing to help pay for new structures and experimental ministries, they have become conservative. The renewal of the church is not an attempt to form another denomination! Renewal is no goal in itself, but is happening for the benefit of the whole church so that the whole church should be a worthy witness to the gospel. If the church (and I write intentionally in the singular) were to take seriously the necessity of its renewal, it would permanently bring together the younger renewers and would force them to work out their experiments practically.[1]

It would, I agree, be disastrous to attempt to integrate in the sense of absorbing or making the new activity, the experimentation, always sufficiently 'convenient' not to disturb the ecclesiastical *status quo*; as though once the would-be innovator had had his fling, worked his spiritual restlessness out of his system, he was expected to revert to type and suffer with the tolerance he had received the exploits of other equally misguided zealots. But integration is possible within a community of tolerance; not the tolerance of self-conscious charity, but the spirit that respects personal integrity and encourages the freedom it demands. It seems to me unrealistic to expect every member of the local church to participate personally in every experiment, or even

[1] *The Humiliation of the Church*, SCM Press 1966, p. 192.

necessarily to approve without serious doubt. A loving and integrated family frequently faces a situation in which one or more of their number feel obligated to follow personal conviction, to follow it without the family's unanimous approval, but always with their united support. The family of the local church is often the same. I have already mentioned how Salvationists at Regent Hall accepted in a spirit of active support experiments of outreach for which they had little time and less personal inclination. They were preoccupied with more traditional activities – an extensive programme of weekly open-air meetings, featuring a brass band of forty-three players and a brigade of fifty-five singers, Sunday-school, youth club, hospital visitation, Bible study groups, and much else – but the young experimenters, seeking for new ways to express their faith, had every reason to know that their efforts were made possible and reinforced by the money, faith, prayers, and general support of virtually everybody. This is not to say that sometimes they did not wish for a greater measure of personal involvement from a greater number or that they were satisfied at the speed of the evolution of change, but they never doubted that they were part of a community. Though they operated outside the existing structures, they never felt outside the fellowship. Though they shared the activities within the structures as little as the average Salvationist shared theirs, and were sometimes as much mystified by the apparent futility of traditional service as the more orthodox were by the new developments, they never doubted the essential oneness of the community to which they belonged. It could well be that groups of Christians will feel obliged to work completely outside existing church structures, to break away almost ostentatiously for the sake of not being encumbered by old associations and misconceptions, but they should still know themselves to be integral members of the church which, whilst respecting their independence, continues ungrudgingly to provide spiritual, moral and financial support. This dream, far from bespeaking fantasy, is already on the way to fulfilment.

What impedes it – and obviously it is impeded for a variety of reasons – is not mainly the confrontation of old reactionaries and young progressives, though this is sometimes problematical enough. The divisions and tensions within the church cut right across age, creating animosity between conservatives and reformers, fundamentalists and liberals, compliants and non-conformists, satisfied and dissatisfied. Teenagers and over-sixties belong to all groups; intolerance is no respecter of persons – youthful bigot or ageing Pharisee. The danger is that members of respective groups tend to gravitate to their own kind, and this explains why local churches are sometimes intolerant of ideas and activities not strictly in harmony with their own. When religious conviction degenerates into fierce dogmatism, it seeks to defend its beliefs against what militant evangelicals almost invariably call 'modernism', a word much used to epitomize teaching with which they disagree. From one standpoint this is good, for strong conviction – without which some of us agree with everybody – is the life-blood of Christianity and clearly needed in a world which often fails to distinguish between tolerance and indulgence; but, like most virtues, it is capable of behaviour brutally at variance with its own authentic spirit.

The community of tolerance I envisage will welcome everybody without trying to impose a common programme of activity, even of worship. To do so would encourage artificiality, the very antithesis of community spirit. It seems to me unrealistic to expect individuals of widely different background and temperament to have common interests, similar capacities, and identical concerns, as unrealistic as to expect the members of a loving family to be exactly the same, or even nearly so, in their tastes and aptitudes. Their unity is more a sense of belonging, of having significance within the group, of *feeling* loved and wanted, than of sharing necessarily the same activities, interests and moral standards. It is to this ideal that the Christian church should move, not accepting people unconditionally only on their confession of faith or insisting that they share a particular mode of worship or join some other form of religious exercise. The church should be a community in which everyone feels at home; accepted, respected as an individual, and given the opportunity to share real relationships. The total community should be inclusive, but incorporate groups with exclusive interests. In other words, the life of the community, its essential vitality, should be these smaller groups, meeting in private homes, church buildings or anywhere convenient, following their own interests – discussion, Bible study, social service, music, drama, sport, transcendental meditation, nothing in particular – without being pressurized to approve of or support personally everybody else's activities. All too often church members are made to feel obligated to take a personal interest in everything centred at the church or organized from it. Equally impossible, they are expected to love every other member of the fellowship, to love them with equal fervour in a manner rare within even the happiest of families. To comfort them in their failings, they are given sermons about loving without liking, and told that love is more intention than fulfilment. Perhaps it is, but this hardly comforts the aspirant after an impossible standard. The Christian community I have in mind will allow its members to work out their own affinities within smaller groups; it will foster relationships of loving mutuality, and by its very nature, the nature of its basic evaluations and aims, widen the possibility of personal fulfilment; its activities, many of them apparently secular and beyond the usual interest of church organization, will serve creative ends and thereby clarify the essential requirements of fulfilment; it will provide traditional forms of worship without making them obligatory, and welcome new expressions of worship without imposing them on all and sundry. Its spirit of tolerance will be tested as experiments are shared in the overlap. For too long the church, in rightly emphasizing the importance of worship, has restricted its meaning to attendance at Sunday services, to participating in officially sanctioned methods of approach to God. These are still meaningful for multitudes of believers, but the inability to make sense of them, to be anything but bored by them, is not in itself evidence that the right attitude of worth-ship is missing. Young people, as we have seen, have it in their social concerns; and the church best helps them to worship in spirit and in truth – to discover Reality and self-fulfilment – by providing them with opportunities to express in practical service their commitment to human need.

This was central, I believe, to the thinking of Harvey Cox when he wrote:

Speaking about God in a secular fashion requires first of all that we place ourselves at those points where the restoring, reconciling activity of God is occurring, where the proper relationship between man and man is

appearing. This means that evangelism, the speaking about God, is political
...To say that speaking of God must be political means that it must
engage people at particular points, not just 'in general'. It must be a
word about their own lives – their children, their jobs, their hopes or dis-
appointments. It must be a word to the bewildering crises within which
our personal troubles arise – a word which builds peace in a nuclear
world, which contributes to justice in an age stalked by hunger, which
hastens the day of freedom in a society stifled by segregation. If the word
is not a word which arises from a concrete involvement of the speaker
in these realities, then it is not a word of God at all but empty twaddle.

We speak of God to secular man by speaking about man, by talking
about man as he is seen in the biblical perspective. Secular talk of God
occurs only when we are participants in that political action by which
he restores men to each other in mutual concern and responsibility. We
speak of God in a secular fashion when we recognize man as his partner,
as the one charged with the task of bestowing meaning and order in
human history.

Speaking of God in secular fashion is thus a political issue. It entails
our discerning where God is working and then joining his work. Standing
in a picket line is a way of speaking. By doing it a Christian speaks of
God. He helps alter the word 'God' by changing the society in which
it has been trivialized, by moving away from the context where 'God-
talk' usually occurs, and by shedding the stereotyped roles in which God's
name is usually intoned. [1]

Exactly! Yet we evangelicals give the impression that God is
confined to church buildings in which alone he can be worshipped
according to prescribed ritual, ritual which varies considerably
with denominational allegiance, but which we insist must be
observed as proof of our Christian commitment. Without wishing
to detract from the importance of worship or to suggest that the
church should not maintain its traditional forms for members that
way inclined, I believe we need to recognize that just as, following Harvey Cox's line, God can be spoken about in indirect ways,
outside the context of religious observance altogether, so he can
be worshipped, he is worshipped, as secular man gives top priority
to the worth-ship of human personality and the things that
enhance it. Dare we say that William Booth, for instance, was
not truly worshipping God when, incensed by the refusal of
match-making factory employers to protect employees from the
possibility of phossy jaw, refused on the grounds that to do so
would inflate costs to bankruptcy level, he started his own factory

---

[1] *The Secular City*, Pelican Books, pp. 265f.

to prove that respect for human personality and profits were not incompatible? Were not the worship of God and worth-ship of people in that case related, the one expressing the other? And was the latter, with its political involvement, any the less worship of God because the 'service' took place outside the customary setting of church and ritual? There can be no doubt, of course, that William Booth and his followers were consciously motivated in their attempts to alleviate human suffering by their love and worship of God, but is similar service less acceptable to him if not motivated in the same way? What if the only conscious motive is the worth-ship of people, the insight that demands fair dealings for every man as a total personality, body, mind and spirit? Surely that is simply another expression of the church's traditional spirit of worship, one in keeping with the aspirations notably of modern youth. They will, I believe, discover the same Reality in their worth-ship of people as we more orthodox believers experience in our deliberate worship of God.

Perhaps I should make it clear that by political involvement I am not referring to *party* politics. The Salvation Army, like organized Christianity in her better moments, has always refused to be identified with any particular political party. It's true that the Church of England has sometimes been described as the Tory Party at prayer, but the very indictment underlines the general recognition that this should not be. The church is above party politics, but deeply involved – or should be – wherever policies adversely impinge upon people, especially those incapable of looking after themselves. This is why the local church, the community of tolerance, to use my favourite description, belongs inalienably to those areas of tension in which housing, rents, racism, and other forms of social injustice await urgent attention. These are the points of human need at which the church should do far more worth-shipping. To do so effectively demands involvement probably in two distinct ways. In the first place the local church as a whole should be immersed in the surrounding community. That's where its roots belong. All too often, alas, it resembles an island in splendid isolation or the headquarters of a secret society. Yet why? Its members care and are keen to work out their Christian discipleship. Individually many of them *are* involved, unself-consciously bearing their witness as good neighbours, trusty employers or employees, trade union leaders, school-teachers, professional social workers, and the like. They are the 'salt' of society, the 'leaven' secretly at work, a source of creative and cleansing influence. This aspect of the local church's involvement is probably under-estimated if not overlooked virtually altogether. It depends upon *being* rather than *doing*, a truth we considered briefly in the previous chapter. But there is still plenty of room for concerted action, doing things together as the Body of Christ, ministering at the crucial points of human need in secular society. Human need sometimes screams for attention, expressing itself in alcoholic, harlot, drug addict, unmarried mother, social misfit. At other times, hiding behind practised modesty or pompous self-sufficiency, it reveals itself in the noisy emptiness of laughter, eyes full of twilight, cynicism (the hand-maid of hurt pride), guilt, self-disparagement, fear, loud gener-osity. Human need is rarely obvious. Its most crude displays are usually symptoms only. Deal with these, a comparatively easy matter, and the disease remains. Keen Christians, particularly those of us who are over-busy, are always in danger of meeting human *need* and not human *persons*. We counsel but have no time to listen. The easy giving of things like money and clothes becomes a substitute for the costly giving of self, an evasion of real encoun-ter. In seeking to overcome this danger, we require each other's help to *see* human need; to see it at depth with Christian insight. Take, for instance, the plight of the mother with a mentally-handicapped child. For twenty-four hours a day, seven days a week, she is never free. The child grows in body, but not in mind; the demands upon the mother, both physical and emotional, are endless. Some local authorities are helping on a growing scale, but rarely in the worst cases. Can the local church do nothing? I am not suggesting that every local church should have a special care unit for mentally-handicapped children, but surely there is room for ecumenical action to this end. There are, of course, many sincere and dedicated evangelicals who deplore such ideas. They argue that the church should preach the gospel, not seek to become an adjunct of the social services. The church, with its dwindling resources of personnel and finance, should, they insist, put first things first and not be side-tracked by deserving but secondary causes. Well, there's room for everybody within a community of tolerance; as the apostle Paul emphasized when he wrote:

> There are different kinds of spiritual gifts, but they are the gifts of the same Spirit. There are different spheres of service, but the service is of the same Lord. There are different kinds of effects, but it is the same God who produces them in every case and in every person. The visible effect which the Spirit produces in each of us is designed for the common good. To one man there is given through the Spirit power to express intellectual wisdom in words; to another by the same Spirit there is given power to communicate knowledge in words. By one and the same Spirit faith is given to one man, and the gift of healing to another; the power to work miracles to another; the gift of prophecy to another; the ability to discern whether or not spirits are from God to another; the gifts of different kinds of ecstatic speech to another; the ability to interpret such speech to another.
>
> It is one and the same Spirit who produces all these different effects, and who, as he wishes, distributes them to each individual person (1 Cor. 12.4-11). [1]

We all have different contributions to make, but always to the same end – that the local church, members of a caring community, should live in the spirit of Christ the servant. He girded himself with a towel and washed the disciples' feet, leaving us, as he said, an example that we should emulate. In my experience this is the major interest of modern youth. Impatient with Christian dogma and doctrine, they nevertheless share Christ's compassion and ask only for the opportunity to prove it. We members of the church, aware of our growing isolation, grieved at the indifference to institutional religion all around us, conscious of the widening gulf that separates us from the people, long for the secret of involvement, of how to overcome our isolation and bridge the gulf of indifference that surrounds our island of apparent irrelevance. That secret, or at least part of it, is, I am convinced, to provide people with the opportunity to share practical service, to share it without their needing first to qualify by confession of faith in what we believe and without being made to feel second-class members of our fellowship until they do confess what we believe. 'It is not permissible,' wrote Paul Tillich in *On the Boundary*,

[1] *The New Testament, Gospels and Acts of the Apostles*, a translation by William Barclay, Collins 1968, p. 55.

to designate as 'un-churched' those who have become alienated from organized denominations and traditional creeds. In living among these groups for half a generation I learned how much of the latent church is within them. I encountered the experience of the finite character of human existence, the quest for the eternal and unconditioned, an absolute devotion to justice and love, a hope that lies beyond any utopia, an appreciation of Christian values and a very sensitive recognition of the ideological misuse of Christianity in the interpenetration of church and state. It has often seemed to me that the 'latent church', as I call what I found among these groups, was a truer church than the organized denominations, if only because its members did not presume to possess the truth.[1]

What practical service could this latent church share? The answer will indicate the extent of the local church's involvement in the community. It could be that we know far too little about the people living on our own doorstep; that the areas of crucial need are foreign to our thinking and beyond our perception; that we have mistaken material prosperity for well-being, and been too readily impressed by appearances of proud independence. Perhaps our first assignment is to discover, helped by the professional social services, the police, probation service, and local voluntary agencies whose ready co-operation is assured, the nature and exact location of need in our community.

This brings me to the second distinctive way in which the local church should possibly be involved. I picked up the seed of the idea at Taizé, in France, the centre for an ecumenical and international religious order whose members make the customary threefold vow of poverty, chastity and obedience, and share a common rule of life, but who are committed to service in the world usually at problem points. The aim is simply Christian presence, the guarantee that committed individuals are living at the grass roots of community life, with time to explore the causes of tension and to seek answers as integral members of that community. Every member of the local church serves to a degree in this direction, but obviously deep involvement is not possible for everybody. By supporting such community-centred activity, activity which probably bears little recognizable relation to organized religion, the local church helps to ensure that its witness grows spontaneously out of the community and

[1] Collins 1967, p. 67.

is not imposed arbitrarily upon it. These cells of Christian presence are particularly needed in central city areas where supporters of the local church are not usually resident in the neighbourhood. Without them, or something similar, the church is bound to become increasingly isolated and finally alien to its own immediate environment.

At Regent Hall we are making a modest effort to move in this direction. Two of our young workers – one of them the leader of our experimental project with young drifters – have moved of their own initiative into Soho, the district in which their work is centred, but they need reinforcing to an extent only possible with ecumenical resources. Meanwhile we continue to seek as a caring community to be involved in the wider community beyond our own doors. Our special care unit for mentally-handicapped children, run entirely by voluntary helpers, is firmly established; the 'Gateway' club for handicapped teenagers is likewise part of our routine programme and supervised by young people; throughout the year groups of shut-ins are conveyed to our hall for a meal and entertainment; each summer car-driver volunteers collect the infirm and take them to Richmond Park before returning to Regent Hall for food and fun. On Christmas Day 200 otherwise lonely people are our guests. They represent many levels of society and are with us in the main for reasons other than material need. We have jazz nights and poetry readings for the young, arrange holidays for sometimes overlooked older people, encourage outings to theatres and other places of interest, organize extensive visitation of hospitals and private homes, put the needy in touch with the needed, engage in discussion and debates, support drama productions and music-making on an ambitious scale, relate young to old, introduce human problems to human answers; in short we cater for specialist groups but foster at every opportunity the sense of belonging to a bigger community of all sorts of people from meths drinkers to middle-class executives. We are obsessed with the idea that the local church is a community or it is nothing; a community of tolerance that accepts everybody, is non-judgmental, never imposes, manipulates, or pushes beyond personal desire, provides opportunities for real relationships, and is outward-looking in all its concerns.

Our conviction is that the vast majority of people need community and can both find personal maturity and make their biggest individual contribution to life only as part of a community. We have a gospel for the strong as well as the weak. All too often the church gives the impression that only when a man is down and almost out does he become a candidate for Christian grace. As though the blatant sinner, the one who indulges the flesh and is categorized as drunkard, adulterer, gambler and the like, is more suited to our evangelical message, being obviously in need of forgiveness and strength, than the man of character with a social conscience. It's true that 'all have sinned and come short of the glory of God', but surely a person does not have to grovel and deny his gifts of integrity and ability before finding a place in the church. The truly strong, Christian and otherwise, are usually the most humble in spirit. They know their limitations and behave accordingly. But they are still strong with so much to offer, despite their lack sometimes of conscious Christian belief and commitment. One of their possible needs is to learn how to translate their qualities of character into strong gentleness, otherwise they go through life intimidating the weak, discouraging the less gifted, and confirming feelings of inferiority in the unsuccessful. There should be no doubt, however, that they have a place in the church and much to contribute to its community of tolerance. We best minister to the strong by providing for them opportunities to minister to the weak. For in the experience of so doing – sharing the perplexities of diverse human need – they gain insight into the mystery and meaning of life, and find God, probably by some other name.

The way forward lies, I believe, in their direction. At the moment they are largely lost to the church through feeling unwanted or fearful that association would involve them in the discipline of formal membership beyond their desires. But many of them belong already in spirit, for – in ways outlined throughout this book – they share the church's aim and share in 'secular' ways the 'essential Christian attitudes of creature to Creator, and of sinner to Saviour'.

# 13

# *Creed and Commitment*

Listening to some preachers, I get the impression that salvation is guaranteed by a mindless acceptance of their understanding of orthodox belief. They reduce the truth to their own verbal gymnastics. Unlike the apostolic company they claim to keep, they see through a glass not darkly, but with the imagined omniscience of God himself. Their understanding of the great imponderables of life and death is closed and stagnant; for them every question-mark of honest inquiry should be a full stop of dogmatism. They give the impression that doubt is sin; that to question traditional definitions of Christian doctrine is blasphemous, a sure stepping-stone to heresy and probably to hell.

I followed Christ long before I believed in him; or should I say I became a Christian – at least in terms of church membership or trying to obey its ethical teaching – long before I clarified my religious beliefs. Initially, Christ was little more than a haunting character or moral influence. He obviously inspired the some-times heroic discipleship of his followers, but for me he was only a figure of history, an object of veneration in an impersonal sort of way. The claim that he was alive and present with those who put their faith in him was bewildering and nonsensical; I thought that such a religion bordered on the superstitious. Nevertheless I was told repeatedly to believe in him. The exhortation only made me more confused and wretched. It was all so vague and unreal. How could I believe? It was like asking me to commit myself to a stranger. In ordinary relationships I believed in people as I got to know them. How could it be otherwise with Jesus Christ? Surely I could not believe *before* I followed. But could I follow before I believed? I searched the New Testament and found what sounded to me like an affirmative answer. Jesus, I noticed, almost never invited people to believe in him; always he gave the invitation, 'Follow me'. It was so with James and John as they washed their nets, and with Peter and Andrew as they cast theirs into the sea. It was so with Matthew as he sat at the receipt of custom, and with the rich young ruler as he sought the secret of eternal life. The same emphasis runs right through the four gospels. The One who told men to love God with all their minds obviously had no intention of imposing upon them definitions of faith against which their reason rebelled. He perceived their doubts; was understanding of their questions. He did not expect them to commit mental suicide in the name of believing faith. 'Follow me,' he said; 'learn of me'. He knew that the following would lead to the learning, and the learning to the believing. So it proved with them – and me.

My decision to become a practising Christian was more an evolution than a revolution. I did not believe in any coherent or articulate way that Jesus was the Son of God; and I had barely heard of the Virgin Birth, the Trinity, the Holy Spirit or much else that goes for essential Christian doctrine. All I can say is that during my twentieth year I became a Christian in a way unknown before. Until then I had attended church, admittedly with progressive infrequency, attempted to pray, spasmodically and never satisfactorily from any standpoint, and in my early teens passed through the inevitable rituals of baptism and confirmation, but religion had been a drag, an unfortunate burden that tended to complicate life and drain it of vitality. I was in the process of ditching it by default when an ecclesiastical canon came along and was bang on target. He was a clergyman of the Church of England, the padre on our RAF station during the second world war. Incredibly, despite compulsory church parades, he was popular. We respected him. We even felt affection for him. His life was more eloquent than his sermons, and they were pretty good most of the time. Sometimes they were spellbinding and always they emphasized that Christianity was a way of life, not a theological argument; that to join the church was to build the kingdom of God, not support a debating society.

We listened often in spite of ourselves. True enough, some of the men were preoccupied with the hymn-number lottery that budding betting-shop tycoons among us always organized, but even

they listened. And unknown to him, his words and – to a greater
extent, I think – his life were disturbing my easy compromise and
smug respectability. That man inspired me to hunger for his faith.
After months of mental turmoil and plodding inquiry, I was still
unsure about his teaching, but I had no doubt about the man himself. He was for me living proof that Christianity worked, that it
gave life significance, purpose, and led to fulfilment. I made the
venture of faith on the basis of his credentials, seeking to live the
Christian life in the hope that questions of doctrine would be
resolved later.

Now this emphasis of doing rather than believing or, more
accurately, of doing as a prelude to believing was surely in the
mind of Jesus when he stated: 'Whoever has the will to do the
will of God shall know whether my teaching comes from him or
is merely my own' (John 7.17, NEB). Dietrich Bonhoeffer said much
the same thing when he wrote: 'Some believe to obey; others
obey to believe.'[1] With the same profound insight, he also said:
'We shall never know what we do not do.'[2] I certainly came to
faith by *doing*; I obeyed to believe. It is true that I thought and
read and argued about the teaching of the church, but essentially
I discovered a living faith by taking just the next step of truth as
I saw it. I read the New Testament or perhaps it would be truer
to say that the New Testament read me. Its pages fascinated,
challenged and inspired me. They introduced me to a world of new
dimensions; lofty idealism, distant goals with immediate practical
implications, bracing discipline, self-forgetful purposes, hopes and
aims undreamt of, peace of mind and joy invulnerable to change.
Everything pulsated with new meaning. The character of Jesus
made sense and captivated me. With increasing frequency he
seemed to step from the obscurity of my doubt and give assurance
to my questing faith. There were many questions unanswered, but
the few answers I did find were more than enough to assure me
that I was moving in the right direction. As with Thomas, my
scepticism was finally defeated, but not, as I have intimated, in one
glorious and unforgettable moment of revelation. I'm not sure
how it happened. All I know is that after months of uncertainty,

[1] *The Cost of Discipleship*, p. 60.
[2] Quoted by Albert H. van den Heuvel in *The Humiliation of the
Church*, p. 112.

of seeking and wondering, I attended a week-end conference about Christian responsibility in a world at war. The talking was not impressive and I've long forgotten what was said, but the fellowship was memorable, indefinable and stimulating. After the final session, I cycled the four miles or so back to the RAF base, and it was then, on that solitary journey, that the realization came to me. Whatever doubts I retained about Christian doctrine, and there were plenty, I was sure that Christ was with me; that indeed he had been with me for some time in ways previously unrealized. It was the Emmaus Road all over again.

My commitment to my understanding of Christian discipleship changed the whole direction of my life, a fact I can't emphasize too strongly. For basically *I* remained the same; my *direction* was changed. There are people, including many of my friends in the Salvation Army, who believe that conversion is primarily a change of character. They point to notorious 'trophies of grace', individuals who have been saved from excessive fleshly indulgences, with all their attendant miseries. Such converts were numerous in the early days of the Salvation Army, and I have met a few myself more recently. But I am still convinced that *they* themselves did not fundamentally change; only their *direction*. God removed their wild excesses, but not the personality inadequacies that caused them in the first place. For just as the grace of God does not save us *from* our troubles but *in* our troubles, so it does not save us *from* our weaknesses but *with* our weaknesses, saves us sometimes so well that our very weaknesses become a means of strength. The Founder of the Salvation Army, William Booth, was unquestionably a spiritual giant, a man whose faith often removed mountains, but all his life he was afflicted with chronic depression, the same aptitude for despondency and dejection that had characterized his earliest days. His conversion at the age of fourteen did not change him in this respect any more than did his implicit faith in God throughout the years. I have known personally 'trophies of grace' who have stopped drinking, gambling, terrorizing their wives and children, but who have remained basically petty and anxious, bombastic or timid. The grace of God did not immediately change them; it changed their direction in life. The distinction is, I believe, important and helps to correct misunderstandings that continue to cause wretchedness for all sorts of

sincere and lovable members of the evangelical church. They have
been led to believe that faith in Christ should instantaneously trans-
form their nature; and when this has not happened they have felt
guilty, rejected and deficient of faith. Yet no one expects, say, a
one-legged man, in consequence of his conversion, to dispense
with his crutches or artificial limb. He will never be able to do so,
but the grace of God will enable him to live victoriously with his
handicap, to make the best of it and even turn it to advantage.
Some of us are handicapped and need crutches in other ways; we
have awkward dispositions and temperaments, a proneness to
anxiety, a conviction of chronic inadequacy; we are full of fear,
sometimes of nothing in particular, of guilt or aggression or
apprehension. We despise ourselves, determine to be different, ask
God to help us, and promise more devoted service in exchange for
deliverance. But we do not change in the depths of our being,
certainly not immediately. It could be, of course, that we need
expert help to understand and come to terms with ourselves.
Undoubtedly the possibility of improving the situation is ours from
a number of sources, not least that represented by our religious
faith and Christian fellowship; but fundamentally we remain what
all the years have made us. God's grace, I reiterate, helps us to
live with and to overcome our limitations and liabilities, rarely to
remove them altogether. However, a fundamental change of
direction in life, which is what conversion is all about, does
initiate a process of change. In our consideration of secular spirituality we noticed that prayer is more directional than devotional.
The two emphases are not mutually contradictory; sometimes they complement each other, but the right direction in thinking, living and desiring is the essential element. In the same way,
salvation is, I believe, the right direction in terms of our evaluations, priorities, and the perspective from which we look at life.
For some people, that direction is guaranteed by faith in Christ,
faith that initiates the believer into a way of life centred in him
and leading to a growing awareness that he is Saviour and Lord. But
with other individuals it is not so straightforward. They find faith
impossible, for a variety of reasons. Told to believe, they ask how
or what, a response sometimes indicating as much the failure of
the church to communicate its gospel intelligibly as the scepticism
of secular society. If commitment to Christian living is dependent

solely upon unconditional acceptance of the Christian creed –
that is, the Christian creed as taught by orthodox believers – then
the majority of secularists are disqualified, a conclusion clearly
disproved by the evidence. There are people of character who
reject Christianity for honourable reasons – intellectual integrity,
fear of all absolute commitments, ignorance or misunderstanding
of church teaching, reluctant lack of faith. Some of them would
like to believe, to accept that Christianity is true, but to them
this seems impossible at the moment. Then has the church nothing
more to say to them? Are they simply rejected as pagans or
heretics and left in the cold of disbelief until, confessing their
errors or ignoring their doubts, they submit to the church's
dogmatism and become orthodox 'believers'? If the answer is yes
– as some sincere Christians insist – the church faces a bleak
future indeed. Its appeal, already seriously waning, will soon be
virtually non-existent. On the other hand, if, as Bonhoeffer suggested, Christian belief is sometimes confirmed and clarified by
Christian action – involvement in meaningful areas of human need
– the church should be offering increasing opportunities for
people – many of them already unconscious 'doers of the word' –
to move in that direction, the direction of practical Christian service. As with me, the creed will take care of itself in the light of
experience.

Secular man is the child of a scientific and technological age, an
age suspicious of authoritarianism and dedicated to authenticity.
The responsibility of the church is to meet him where he is, and to
share with him, as well as be prepared to learn from him, the
truth that sets men free. For God's will is that all men should
have the opportunity to be themselves and to fulfil their potential
as total human beings. To attempt this along the lines suggested
is for evangelicals to risk misunderstanding, misrepresentation, and
even opposition in the name of religion; it is to venture, like
Abraham, into a far country, knowing the way but not immediately the final destination. Doubtless, many mistakes will be made
and wrong turnings taken. Possibly, good people, convinced that
evangelical truth lies in another direction altogether, will be hurt
and provoked to fierce condemnation. But in the final analysis
what matters most is our motivation; not *what* we do, but *why*
we do it. For God alone knows our hearts and desires, our hopes

and aims, the reason behind our deeds. We stand before him, condemned only by our refusal to walk in the light of the truth we perceive. Some of us obey because we believe; others believe because we obey. Either way, as Dietrich Bonhoeffer's last testimony reminds us, with God every apparent end is only a more glorious new beginning.

# Index